Going
Raw

First published in the United States of America by
Quarry Books, a member of
Quarto Publishing Group USA Inc.
100 Cummings Center
Suite 406-L
Beverly, Massachusetts 01915-6101
Telephone: (978) 282-9590
Fax: (978) 283-2742
www.quarrybooks.com

Library of Congress Cataloging-in-Publication Data
Wignall, Judita.
 Going raw : everything you need to start your own raw food diet and lifestyle revolution at home / Judita Wignall.
     p. cm.
 Includes index.
 ISBN-13: 978-1-59253-685-6
 ISBN-10: 1-59253-685-9
 1. Vegetarian cooking. 2. Vegetarianism. 3. Raw foods. 4. Raw food diet. 5. Cookbooks. I. Title.
 TX837.W47 2011
 641'5'636—dc22

                                                            2010046970

ISBN-13: 978-1-59253-685-6
ISBN-10: 1-59253-685-9

15

Design: Rita Sowins / Sowins Design
Photography and cover image: Matt Wignall
Food styling: Sienna DeGovia
To access online content go to www.quarrybooks.com/pages/going_raw

Printed in China

The information in this book is for educational purposes only. It is not intended to replace the advice of a physician or medical practitioner. Please see your health care provider before beginning any new health program.

BEVERLY MASSACHUSETTS

QUARRY BOOKS

Going Raw

Everything You Need to Start Your Own
RAW FOOD DIET & Lifestyle Revolution at Home

Judita Wignall

Photography by Matt Wignall

Contents

Contents

Foreword by Cherie Soria, Living Light Culinary Institute   6

Introduction   8

Chapter 1: Why Go Raw?   10
Rules of the Raw Road   11
Nutritional Basics of Raw Food   14
The Benefits of Raw Food   17
The Cost of Eating Raw   22
Living Green, Living Compassionately   24

Chapter 2: Raw Basics   26
Stocking Your Pantry   27
The Tools   31
Basic Knife Skills   35
Using a Mandoline   38
Raw Techniques   41
Think like a Chef   52

Chapter 3: Recipes for the Revolution   54
Smoothies   56
Juices   62
Breakfast   64
Salads and Dressings   71

Soups and Sides   86
Entrées   103
Desserts   130
Snacks   149
Beverages   158
Living and Fermented Foods   162
Quick and Easy Extras   168
Quick and Easy Bites, Savory   170
Quick and Easy Bites, Sweet   172

Chapter 4: Successfully Raw   174
How Much Raw Is Right for You?   175
Easy Raw Tips and Tricks   178
Meal Planning   179
Sample 7-Day Menu   180
Looking at Health Holistically   182

Glossary   187
Resources   189
Index   190
Acknowledgments   192
About the Author   192
About the Photographer   192

Foreword by Cherie Soria
Living Light Culinary Institute

We are in the midst of a revolution in health consciousness thanks to pioneers, such as Judita Wignall, who have discovered the benefits of the raw food diet and are passionately sharing it with others. This revolution promotes a natural way of living that can enable us to experience improved health and general well-being, weight loss, increased energy and stamina, reduced allergies, improved digestion, prevention and reversal of disease, and a more positive attitude about life.

Adding more raw, plant-based foods to your diet can also help preserve the well-being of the creatures of the earth and, indeed, the earth itself. For those interested in reducing our carbon footprint, changing to a raw food diet will do more than recycling and driving an electric car, combined! In the process, you will also spare the lives of countless animals.

The fact that the raw food diet is a health-promoting lifestyle for humans, animals, and the planet, however, is not enough to gain favor with people unless it also tastes great. We are accustomed to eating for flavor, texture, appearance, and comfort—so no matter how good food is for us, if it doesn't feed us emotionally we will not eat it … at least not for long. One would have to be on death's door to eat food that is flavorless and uninteresting. Even then, most people continue to eat the foods that bring them comfort, even when those foods are killing them! That's why it is so important to make healthful foods taste as good as or better than the cooked foods people are accustomed to eating, and why this book is so important. *Going Raw* showcases the kind of foods that will delight you while you also improve your health and general well-being. It will teach you the benefits of the raw food diet and inspire you to eat it for enjoyment as well as for health and vitality.

Best of all, Judita has made it easy for you to follow along with the recipes by providing step-by-step photos so you know exactly what to do from start to finish. This is an exquisitely beautiful book that is unique in its approach. Judita wants you to be successful and has gone to great lengths to make sure you can create delicious meals for yourself and your family. You will find plenty of compelling information about why the raw food diet is superior to other ways of eating and how to get started on a raw path.

I first met Judita when she attended our culinary arts institute, Living Light, in Fort Bragg, California. At Living Light we teach people from all walks of life to make healthy living delicious, and Judita has certainly proved herself adept at carrying that mission forward. Her creativity, professionalism, and determination to bring the benefits of raw cuisine to the world are the keystones of her work in *Going Raw*.

If you are overweight and seeking permanent weight loss, or just want to achieve better health and more energy without giving up the enjoyment of tasty, satisfying, nurturing meals, the raw food diet is for you. It emphasizes sensible, plant-based nutrition and offers what few diets can: a way to bring your weight into balance while you simultaneously become healthier and happier. This is a diet for life—not just one that you stay with until you lose weight.

Going Raw will teach you a sustainable way of eating that has the potential to become a thoroughly enjoyable lifestyle. The raw food diet is loaded with the nutrients your body needs to fight disease, lose weight, and be optimally healthy. It has all the protein, vitamins, minerals, phytochemicals, and antioxidants you need to build a vibrant body.

The best part is you do not have to eat 100 percent raw foods 100 percent of the time to maintain good health—so don't be afraid to get started today. Begin with a few of the easy-to-prepare recipes depicted in *Going Raw* and taste for yourself why so many people around the world are embracing a diet high in raw vegan foods. Join the raw food revolution—you'll be glad you did!

—**CHERIE SORIA**, founder and director, Living Light Culinary Institute
coauthor, *Raw Food Revolution Diet*, with Brenda Davis, RD, and Vesanto Melina, RD
www.RawFoodChef.com

Introduction

The responses people give me when I mention that I'm raw are always interesting.
No meat? No cooked food? Where do you get your protein? What do you eat? I really don't
mind the inquisition because I love to share my dietary views with anyone interested in hearing them. I was the inquisitor years ago when I was struggling to find a natural cure for my
acne. I was an actress and a model in Hollywood and had acne like the city had traffic. I needed a solution to my skin problems and was open to anything, even something that seemed as
crazy as not cooking my food. I quickly discovered the transformative power of eating foods
that heal. Eating for energy. Eating to live.

In one month of eating 100 percent raw I lost 15 pounds, eliminated my arthritis, and lifted
my depression. I had energy through the roof and a mental clarity I had not experienced in
years. In three months my skin cleared up, and I just couldn't bring myself to go back to my old
way of eating microwaved pouches of food squeezed onto my dinner plate.

I was in love with raw foods. I loved the texture, the freshness—the living energy was in-
toxicating. I admit I missed some of the favorites from my previous "standard American diet".
I decided that a great way to keep things interesting was to buy every raw food recipe book
available. When I finished reading those, I went to Living Light Culinary Institute to become
a raw food chef. I started studying holistic nutrition, and soon I was teaching Raw Food 101
classes. I started a blog, filmed videos, and then compiled a book of original recipes. I became a
woman with a message and a purpose. Pretty radical for someone who used to hate cooking.

I wrote this book to demystify raw foods and to help make the raw food lifestyle accessible
and simple. Whether you are looking to go all raw or just replace some of your junk food with
healthier fare, I offer you plenty of options here to get you started. I can't promise it's the fast-
est food you'll ever make, but I can tell you it is some of the tastiest you'll ever eat. I've photo-
graphed all of the essential steps of several food preparation techniques so you never have to
wonder if you're doing it right. There are fast and easy recipes in *Going Raw* as well as some
gourmet dishes for true raw food enthusiasts. From the delicious recipes to the culinary tips
and tricks to the nutritional tidbits, this book will equip and inspire you to start your own raw
food revolution at home.

In going raw there are no hard and fast rules—just the adventure of eating foods in a whole
new way.

Eat well and be well!

-Judita

Chapter 1 | # Why Go Raw?

Raw food is fresh, whole food that has not been refined, chemically processed, denatured, or heated above 118°F (48°C), so its nutritional content is preserved. The major raw food groups are fruits, vegetables, sprouted seeds, nuts, grains, sea vegetables, and natural fats. People who eat a raw food diet are called *raw foodists.*

Fundamentally, raw food is not a new concept. Most of us have grown up hearing various government or health organizations tell us we need to eat several servings of fruits and vegetables a day. When we eat foods in their natural, uncooked state we receive all the vitamins, minerals, phytonutrients, and enzymes Mother Nature intended for us. When we cook our foods, we can lose around 70 percent of these essential nutrients.

Rules of the Raw Road

* **Some raw foodists eat animal products such as raw dairy, meat, sushi, eggs, honey, and bee pollen.**

* **Most raw foodists are vegans (which means they don't consume any animal products).** They may be "beegans" (because they consume bee products but no other animal products).

* **Frozen fruit is considered raw (though it does lose about 30 percent of its nutrient content), but vegetables, which are blanched, or boiled, before being frozen, are not.**

* **Anything canned or pasteurized is not raw.** Most canned foods have been heated to around 250°F (116°C) and then sit on store shelves for months. Most of these cans are lined with a plastic coating that leaches BPA, an estrogenic chemical compound that has been shown to disrupt the endocrine system, affecting fertility as well as brain and behavior development in children, and can lead to cancer, diabetes, and other diseases. Pasteurization is a process that heats juices, milk, and dairy products to at least 145°F (63°C) (flash pasteurization occurs at 161°F [72°C]) for three minutes. This is to kill any harmful bacteria, but it unfortunately destroys the enzymes and some of the nutritional value.

Some raw vegans abstain from animal products for ethical reasons, while some believe that humans were made to eat only plants. This belief is based upon the naturalist view that our closest relative in the animal kingdom, the African bonobo primate, lives on a diet of mostly green leaves and fruit. We share about 99 percent of our DNA with the bonobo and have similar physiology. Our teeth and digestive systems are much closer to theirs than to carnivores', who have sharper teeth and claws, very acidic stomach juices, and shorter digestive tracts—perfect for eating animal flesh.

Most raw foodists thrive on just raw plant food, while some fare better when they include small amounts of raw animal products such as raw dairy and eggs. Everyone has different nutritional needs, so there are no hard and fast rules. Over time, you will learn to be in tune with your body's needs, and what degree of raw makes it sing.

This book contains recipes that are entirely plant based except for a few that call for ethically cultivated raw honey and bee pollen. You could call this book raw beegan.

THE RAW FOOD GROUPS

This is not an exhaustive list but an overview of many of the delicious ingredients that you can enjoy on a raw food diet.

* **Fruits:** apples, oranges, strawberries, pineapples, papaya, bananas, apricots, plums, dates, and dried fruits, just to name a few. Fruits are loaded with vitamins and carbohydrates to fuel our cells.

* **Vegetables:** cucumbers, celery, bell peppers, tomatoes, beets, zucchini, broccoli, cauliflower, peas, corn, and so on. Vegetables are low in calories and full of fiber, so you can eat as much as you like. Potatoes and hard squashes are difficult to eat raw, but some raw foodists find them palatable.

* **Leafy greens:** green and red leaf lettuce, kale, spinach, Swiss chard, romaine, bok choy, watercress, arugula, dandelion, and lambsquarters. Green leaves are essential to a raw food diet because they are a great source of protein and contain essential minerals such as calcium, iron, and magnesium.

* **Seeds:** pumpkin, sunflower, hemp, flax, chia, and sesame are a great source of protein and essential minerals.

* **Nuts:** almonds, cashews, Brazil nuts, walnuts, pecans, pine nuts, hazelnuts, pistachios, raw wild jungle peanuts, and macadamia nuts.

* **Grains:** oats, kamut, spelt, buckwheat, and hand-parched wild rice.

* **Sprouts:** alfalfa, sunflower, broccoli, clover, mung beans, chickpeas, lentils, and quinoa are just a few types of sprouts you can grow at home. (See page 48 for sprouting instructions.)

* **Fermented foods:** sauerkraut, coconut kefir, coconut yogurt, rejuvelac, and miso paste. Fermented foods contain high amounts of beneficial bacteria that help improve our digestion and strengthen our immune system.

* **Fats:** avocados, coconuts, and sun-dried olives as well as oils such as coconut, flaxseed, hemp seed, and olive. Make sure they are cold-pressed (not expeller-pressed) and extra virgin. Avoid peanut oil, which may cause allergic reactions. Also avoid canola, soybean, and corn oil, because they are usually very processed and may come from genetically modified crops.

* **Sea vegetables:** There are at least two dozen edible seaweeds, but my favorites are dulse, kelp, nori, wakame, and arame. They are a great substitute for salt and full of essential trace minerals.

* **Superfoods:** Superfoods have exceptionally high concentrations of nutrients and unique properties. There are many out there, but my favorites are goji berries, maca powder, bee pollen, blue-green algae, marine phytoplankton, and cacao.

* **Sweeteners:** clear agave nectar, palm sugar, raw honey, dried stevia leaf, yacon syrup, mesquite powder, maple syrup, and dehydrated cane juice (rapadura). Except for raw honey, stevia leaf, and mesquite, most sugars are processed to some extent and are not considered truly raw, even if they are labeled as such. Avoid white processed sugar, sugar in the raw, and turbinado sugar, which are all stripped of their minerals. Also steer clear of all artificial sweeteners such as aspartame, sucralose, and saccharin.

Nutritional Basics of Raw Food

Cooking depletes the nutritional content of our food by damaging the nutrients and vitality of the food and at the same time making it more difficult to assimilate the remaining nutrients. At 113°F to 118°F (45°C to 48°C) the enzymes begin to break down and lose their catalytic power. At around 135°F (57°C) we destroy the vitamins and phytonutrients (antioxidants). Minerals are not affected by heat, but if we boil our food, minerals will be lost in the water.

Another perspective on heating our food: Human skin burns and our skin cells die at about 130°F (54°C).

At around 160°F (71°C) the sugars in carbohydrate-rich foods, such as potatoes and grain products, begin to caramelize, making them less effective as an energy source.

Cooked vegetables have lost much of their fiber content, which makes them less effective at sweeping out the digestive system.

THE PERILS OF PROCESSED FOOD

At no other time in history have humans had a diet so full of altered foods. The grocery store shelves are stocked with processed foods that have been stripped of almost all their nutrients and contain substances completely foreign to our bodies, such as MSG and trans fats. The definition of processed food used in this book is anything that was man-made in a factory with altered or refined ingredients and packaged to sit on store shelves for weeks or months. This applies not just to chips and cookies, but also includes "instant" meals you heat in the microwave or add water to. Even unassuming whole grain cereals and muffins are processed foods. Many of them are filled with preservatives, sodium, artificial flavors and colorings, and hydrogenated oils and contain corn and soy fillers, most of which are genetically modified.

The irony of this modern diet is that people who eat only processed foods can eat upward of 4,000 calories a day and still be extremely deficient in vitamins and minerals. This deficiency may drive us to graze all day on junk food yet never feel satisfied. Adding nutrient-rich raw food to your diet can calm cravings, balance mood swings, increase energy, strengthen the immune system, and help with weight loss.

Domesticated animals that eat the processed foods humans feed them will eventually develop some of the same dietary illnesses that plague humans, such as arthritis, obesity, diabetes, and cancer. My cat, Arlo, became extremely obese and almost died from complications related to eating store-bought cat food. Now he thrives on a raw meat diet.

THE COOKING COMPROMISE

Another issue that arises from cooking food is that certain toxins and carcinogens are formed when high heat is used. Heated high-fat, high-protein animal foods create advanced glycation end products (AGEs), which have been shown to increase blood pressure, create wrinkles in the skin, and accelerate aging. Heating starches with oils (as when making french fries, potato chips, breads, cookies, and crackers) creates acrylamides, substances known to cause cancer in laboratory animals. Whenever you see food that is browned, such as a loaf of bread, that is acrylamide.

Cooking meat creates heterocyclic amines (HCAs), another carcinogenic compound. HCAs are most abundant in well-done, fried, and barbecued meats and have been linked to stomach, pancreatic, colorectal, and breast cancers according to the National Cancer Institute. When you imagine how frequently most people consume these foods—on a daily basis, week after week, year after year—it is no surprise that cancer cases continue to rise.

Cooked Food and the Immune System

A landmark example of the effect of cooked food on the immune system came to light in the 1930s. A Swiss scientist, Dr. Paul Kouchakoff, studied the effect of digestive leukocytosis, a well-known phenomenon in which white blood cell count rises after eating. Dr. Kouchakoff conducted more than three hundred experiments showing that leukocytosis does not occur when one eats raw foods but creates a very strong response after eating cooked, canned, and especially processed foods. He renamed it pathological leukocytosis because the body's reaction to a foreign invader causes the increase in white blood cell count.

TEA, COFFEE, AND ALCOHOL

Most tea leaves are dried at high temperatures and steeped in hot water, so they do not fall into the raw category, but many raw foodists still drink herbal teas for their medicinal properties. Some herbs, such as horsetail and nettles, contain great bone-building minerals, while chanca piedra may be helpful in breaking up kidney stones and gallstones. Some teas are made with medicinal mushrooms, spices, and roots and are considered by some raw food leaders to be powerful immune boosters and as important as raw foods.

Black tea, green tea, white tea, and yerba maté contain caffeine, which most raw foodists avoid. (I do not drink caffeinated tea very often, but when I need a little boost I reach for organic white tea). Most raw foodists avoid coffee. It disrupts sleep patterns, makes the body acidic, can exhaust the adrenal system, has to be detoxified through the liver, and is a false source of energy. It is also dehydrating and causes mineral loss. Try to wean yourself from your daily coffee dependence and allow raw foods to give you the energy you need. I was a devout coffee addict before I went raw, and I can attest that I have more energy now than when I drank it.

Most hardcore raw foodists do not imbibe much alcohol because of its acidity and the fact that it is taxing on the liver. For people who spend years working toward optimum health, putting something toxic into the body is a step backward. That does not mean the party has to end for you, though, so to speak. Assess your health and see if the benefits you reap personally from alcohol consumption are worth it. I personally enjoy a drink on occasion and see no harm if alcohol is consumed in moderation. Since red wine and sake are both fermented, they're technically considered raw. Look for organic wines with no sulfates added. I have included a classic red sangria recipe that makes a great warm-weather cooler. As with everything, use alcohol in moderation, to whatever quantities work with your body and your lifestyle.

······························· ✺ ·······························

More athletes have turned to plant-based whole foods to fuel their activity in the last few years than in the previous fifteen. Because it works. Plant-based protein sources are more alkaline-forming than their animal counterparts. Increased alkalinity directly translates to greater muscle functionality, and therefore improved efficacy of movement. Quicker recovery after exercise is also a significant factor. Faster recovery after training will allow for workouts to be scheduled closer, and therefore more will be done in a shorter amount of time. This directly translates to greater performance.

—Brendan Brazier, pro Ironman triathlete, author of Thrive,
and formulator of sport performance supplement Vega

The Benefits of Raw Food

When you begin to incorporate raw foods into your daily diet, big changes start to happen in your body. The more raw food you add, the bigger the benefits. Here are just a few of the things you can start to notice immediately, just by adding a few servings of raw foods each day.

* **Raw foods are energizing.** Most people notice their energy levels increasing when they eat raw. Raw foods are much easier to digest than a big steak or a bean and cheese burrito. Raw foods are less dense than starchy or processed food, but they also contain enzymes, protein catalysts that help our digestion by breaking down food into smaller parts. This puts less strain on the body to produce its own digestive enzymes.

* **Raw foods are hydrating.** This can help us with sluggishness, dry skin, and false hunger that can occur when we don't consume enough water.

* **Raw foods help boost our immune system.** Many people claim to get sick less frequently after incorporating more raw foods into their diet. Some of this has to do with pathogenic leukocytosis mentioned earlier. Our white blood cells are free to fight real pathogens such as cold viruses. Raw foods also contain copious amounts of vitamin C, beta carotene, and zinc, three very powerful immune boosters. Personally, I haven't had a cold or the flu in years, and my seasonal allergies are much better since switching to a raw food diet.

* **Raw foods contain loads of fiber.** Fiber is essential for sweeping the digestive tract of waste. Many health problems, such as simple gas and bloating, can stem from poor digestion, but irritable bowel syndrome, yeast infections, poor nutrient absorption, skin conditions such as acne, and even colon cancer can also result. According to Donna Gates, author of *The Body Ecology Diet*, your immune system is intimately connected to the health of your gut, so it's important to pay attention to it. Make sure you're "moving things along" at least once a day, but ideally after each meal.

* **Raw foods contain phytonutrients.** These are plant chemical compounds that act as antioxidants, immune boosters, and hormone stabilizers and can offer us many health benefits, such as detoxifying the liver, preventing heart disease and cancer, and protecting our eyes from macular degeneration. Lycopene is a well-known phytonutrient found in red fruits and vegetables such as tomatoes, watermelons, red bell peppers, and papayas and has very powerful antioxidant properties. Research suggests lycopene is effective in preventing cancers, especially prostate, lung, and stomach cancer. Resveratrol is another popular phytonutrient found in red grapes that has been linked to heart health. There are thousands of other phytonutrients out there and thousands still yet to be discovered by scientists.

✳

Our bodies are constantly in a state of healing. If we cut our skin, our body immediately starts healing the wound. If we are exposed to a virus, our white blood cells go on the warpath to fight it, and we may be completely unaware of it.

The process of digesting food is the most complex job our body does, and it has to do it several times a day. It is so complex that the body's process of healing pauses when food is digesting. When we eat a simple, easy-to-digest diet of raw foods, our body has more energy to fight pathogens, rebuild tissue, and detoxify.

Raw Nutrition

Fortunately, plant based nutrition is becoming more accepted into the mainstream. It seems that almost every day a new study comes out about the benefits of raw foods. Here are a few of the basics that are important to know as you dive in.

Raw Sources of Protein

One of the biggest concerns people have about following a plant-based diet is whether they will get enough protein. The good news is that all plants contain protein, especially green leafy vegetables. Green leafy vegetables such as kale, spinach, parsley, collard greens, arugula, and so on are composed of 35 to 50 percent protein. Other good-quality sources of protein include hemp seeds, chia seeds, goji berries, cacao, almonds, bee pollen, spirulina, blue-green algae, chlorella,

SOURCES OF VEGETABLE PROTEIN (PER SERVING)

	SERVING SIZE	PROTEIN
Hemp seeds	1 ounce	10 grams
Almonds	¼ cup	7 grams
Buckwheat	1 cup	6 grams
Chia seeds	¼ cup	6 grams
Cacao nibs	1 ounce	4 grams
Goji berries	1 ounce	4 grams
Kale	1 cup	2.5 grams
Spinach	1 cup	2 grams

pumpkin seeds, sprouts, sprouted grains, sprouted wild rice, and vegetable powders. Eating a variety of foods every day can provide a sufficient amount of protein. If you are an athlete or are pregnant, you can easily increase your protein intake by taking measures such as adding more hemp seeds to your salad or smoothie or eating a small handful of almonds.

Leafy Greens and Chlorophyll

Leafy greens contain chlorophyll, the substance that gives plants their green pigment. The molecular structure of chlorophyll is almost identical to the hemoglobin in our blood. While the center atom of hemoglobin is iron, the center atom of chlorophyll is magnesium. This similar composition allows chlorophyll to actually help rebuild and replenish our blood cells while delivering much-needed oxygen to our tissues. It also acts as a chelator, which pulls toxic heavy metals from our body and has anticarcinogenic properties, protecting against cancer-causing substances such as cooked meat toxins and air pollution. Starting your day with Our Daily Greens (see page 63) will help you feel energized, and you can be assured you've gotten a big boost of alkalizing minerals, oxygen, and enzymes.

* * *

A great way to get the maximum nutritional benefit from green leaves is to blend them into smoothies. Blending the greens breaks down the tough cellular walls so that we can better assimilate their nutrients. Victoria Boutenko, a longtime raw foodist and author, is the pioneer of the green smoothie movement. She has written two great books about the importance of green leaves in our diets, including the highly recommended *Green for Life.* (See "Resources" on page 189.)

THE PROBLEMS WITH SOY

In the vegan culinary world, soy is a major protein staple. Products such as tofu, textured vegetable protein (which is an essential part of imitation meat), and soy milk have been heated and processed and are not a part of the raw food diet. A lot of controversy also surrounds the health benefits of soy. Though it is high in protein, it also contains phytoestrogens and various toxins that can have a profound effect on the thyroid and the hormonal development of children, as well as a host of other health problems.

In addition, most nonorganic soybeans are genetically modified organisms (GMOs) and have yet-unknown health risks. There is reason to believe GMOs can cause allergic reactions, infertility, and metabolic disruptions, and may be linked to liver failure. The best sources of soy are fermented soy products such as tempeh, miso, and traditionally brewed soy sauces such as tamari and nama shoyu.

Tempeh is not consumed by most people in the raw world because it has to be cooked (usually fried or blackened), but miso paste and soy sauces are often used as seasonings in raw food recipes. I prefer chickpea miso to soy-based miso, both of which can be found in the refrigerator section of many health food stores.

True tamari is wheat/gluten free (check the label before buying), while nama shoyu is unpasteurized, making it more popular with the raw purists. For people with soy allergies or those who prefer to omit soy from their diet, companies like Coconut Secret make fermented soy-free soy sauce from the sap of coconut trees. For my recipes, I like to use tamari, but feel free to use your favorite and adjust the seasoning if needed.

Raw Sources of Calcium

Green leafy vegetables are a great source of bioavailable calcium, as are unhulled sesame seeds (or raw tahini), kale, collards, broccoli, bok choy, endive, kelp, and figs.

For proper calcium absorption, be sure to get adequate sunlight exposure every day (about ten to fifteen minutes a day) or take a vitamin D_3 supplement. It's also important to eat foods that contain silica and magnesium, such as pumpkin seeds, spinach, apples, oranges, cherries, cucumber, onions, beets, celery, almonds, bananas, figs, buckwheat, and cacao. These foods assist in building up and maintaining bone density. Magnesium and silica can also be found in horsetail and nettle tea.

Raw Sources of Iron

The body handles iron from plants slightly differently than it handles iron from meat. Our bodies will only absorb as much plant-derived iron as it needs and will eliminate the excess. This is a good thing. Iron toxicity can cause free-radical damage and is associated with Alzheimer's disease, colorectal cancer, liver cancer, and an increased risk of heart disease. Iron-rich foods include pumpkin seeds, sesame seeds, sunflower seeds, kale, romaine lettuce, kelp, broccoli, bok choy, and herbs such as basil, thyme, dill, parsley, and oregano.

Importance of B_{12}

B_{12} is an essential vitamin created by bacteria and cobalt found in the soil. Grazing animals are a good source of B_{12}, but because of mineral-depleted topsoil, animals and humans are becoming B_{12} deficient. Farmers fortify their animals' diets with B_{12} supplements, and if you're a vegan or vegetarian a good supplement is essential, too. I suggest a transdermal patch or a sublingual supplement of methylcobalamin, the most bioavailable form. B_{12} deficiency can cause fatigue, memory loss, anemia, depression, and irreversible nerve and neurological damage. We carry a three-year supply of B_{12} in our livers, but it's important to supplement before it's too late.

HOW RAW SHOULD YOU GO?

You don't need to be a vegetarian or vegan to go raw, nor do you need to be 100 percent raw to reap many of the diet's benefits. Any amount of raw food is beneficial, but try to aim for a 50 percent raw diet to feel a notable difference. Think about it this way: If you add just a smoothie to your morning routine and a salad before lunch and dinner, you're already there!

Many people choose to go 100 percent raw as a way to deeply detox and have incredible results. Angela Stokes-Monarch, a raw food author and speaker, went through a radical transformation when she went raw. Suffering from an underactive thyroid and weighing almost 300 pounds, she started a raw food diet and lost 160 pounds in two years. Though she began at 100 percent raw, she went down to a 70 percent raw diet in the first year and still maintained a deep detox.

* * *

In the documentary film *Simply Raw: Reversing Diabetes in 30 Days*, six people with diabetes went on a 100 percent raw diet, and within two weeks each one was able to drastically reduce or eliminate his or her insulin needs. It's a very powerful example of the restorative, healing power of a good diet.

* * *

Besides significant weight loss, people have reported arthritis elimination, lifting of depression, removal of arterial plaque, and reduction of the need for insulin. All of these conditions, which are caused by a poor diet, can be helped and possibly reversed by following a healthy diet of fresh, raw foods.

Making the Change

Try incorporating raw foods into your diet gradually, and only as much as you are comfortable with. Going 100 percent raw overnight can create a very rapid detoxing effect on your body. Headaches, irritability, and fatigue are common if your diet changes faster than your body can adjust to it.

As you add more raw foods and let go of the processed foods, you may experience withdrawals and massive cravings for these foods. Be strong—it's only temporary! It is well worth the effort in the long run to overcome addiction to food that is less than beneficial to our bodies.

Always keep in mind: It isn't all or nothing with raw foods. There's no gold medal waiting for you if you reach 100 percent raw. The core goal—for everyone—is to eat sensibly and give your body the best-quality food you can.

The Cost of Eating Raw

It's a strange world when buying a few pieces of fresh produce is more expensive than two large pizzas or a family-sized bucket of chicken wings. The reason fast food and processed food are so cheap is because much of it is government subsidized. According to the Physicians Committee for Responsible Medicine, the U.S. government spends about 73 percent of its agricultural subsidies budget on meat and dairy and another 13 percent on grains, while less than 1 percent goes to helping produce farmers.

Processed foods are also made with the cheapest ingredients on the planet: wheat, corn, and soy. These three ingredients are in almost all processed foods and go by many different aliases (see sidebar at right).

Cheap food is just that—cheap and low grade. Eating these foods may affect your health in the long run by leading to health problems such cardiovascular disease, diabetes, osteoporosis, or even cancer. By purchasing the best food you can afford, you are investing in good health for the long term. You are worth the investment!

That being said, not all raw foods are expensive. **Farmers' markets** not only have the freshest foods you can buy, but also farmers will often give you a deal if you buy food in bulk. Find friends with whom you can buddy up on big purchases. Buy your fruit in bulk and freeze the excess to use in smoothies or thaw for use later. Another way you can save on produce is by becoming a member of a **CSA** (community supported agriculture). This is a great way to get produce fresh from the farmer when it comes into season. Urbanites can also sign up for weekly food delivery services that drop off boxes of produce from local farms. It's less expensive and better quality than the grocery stores and will save you from an extra shopping trip every week.

Finally, you can always **grow your own food**. If you have the space and a little bit of time, small-space or container gardening will generate a lot of results with minimal investment. Nothing beats a fresh tomato salad made entirely of ingredients you grew yourself! (See "Resources" on page 189.)

BUYING ORGANIC

Organic foods cost more than conventionally grown foods, but their flavor is often superior, and they are free of cancer-causing pesticides and fungicides. Some foods are more heavily sprayed than others, so if you can afford only a few organic items on your shopping list, then choose wisely.

You should always buy organic strawberries, apples, celery, bell peppers, spinach, cherries, blueberries, nectarines, kale, peaches, cantaloupe, apricots, green beans, grapes, and cucumbers.

WHEAT, SOY, CORN: OTHERWISE KNOWN AS ...

* Wheat: gelatinized starch, gluten, hydrolyzed vegetable protein, starch, triticale, triticum aestivum, vegetable gum, vegetable starch, vital gluten, wheat bran, wheat germ, wheat gluten, wheat malt, wheat starch, gum arabic

* Soy: bulking agent, emulsifier, guar gum, hydrolyzed vegetable protein (HVP), lecithin, monosodium glutamate (MSG), protein, protein extender, soy flour, soy panthenol, soy protein, soy protein isolate or concentrate, soybean oil, stabilizer, starch, textured vegetable protein (TVP), thickener, vegetable broth, vegetable starch

* Corn: high fructose corn syrup (HFCS), corn sugar, corn syrup, corn syrup solids, cornstarch, crystalline fructose, crystalline glucose, dextrose, glucose, glucose syrup, lecithin (from corn), maltodextrin

These are the most heavily sprayed foods (according to the Environmental Working Group). You should also beware of organic foods that are imported from outside your home country, because other countries' standards may differ from what you are accustomed to. Whichever route you go, always clean your fruits and vegetables well with a good produce wash before eating.

Living Green, Living Compassionately

A raw food diet helps you live a more environmentally friendly life in many ways. Because raw foods don't come with much packaging, you are not generating a lot of waste. Plus, if you can incorporate buying local produce into your raw food lifestyle, you will contribute to fewer trucks on the roads, generate a smaller carbon footprint, and support local farmers. Your food scraps, such as kale stems or zucchini skins, can be either juiced or composted. Nothing goes to waste in the raw food life!

In addition to being environmentally sound, adopting a plant-based diet is compassionate. Eating less meat means you participate in less animal suffering. The conditions for animals raised in factory farms are very sad. Animals are packed in so densely, they barely move more than a few inches their entire lives. Many stand in their own manure and never see daylight. Chickens have their beaks clipped because they go mad and attack each other. They are fed unnatural diets and must be given antibiotics to survive in their deplorable conditions. This is not intended to be preachy, but it's the hard truth behind raising animals for mass consumption.

If we can get most of our nutrients from plants, why not choose to minimize animal suffering? If you enjoy meat and eggs, buy grass-fed meats and pastured eggs from farmers who have made commitments to raising their animals more compassionately.

This holds true for other consumer purchases we make as well. Buying cruelty-free clothing, accessories, and cosmetics is not only good for the conscience but good for the environment.

· ✳ ·

Somebody once said, "You are what you eat." Although I've never considered myself a potato or a bean, I certainly feel better knowing that my existence is a result of a plant-based food chain rather than the product of the slaughterhouse. Organic produce, carefully grown and inventively prepared, provides a wonderfully nutritious diet that's both healthy and complete.

—*quarrygirl, from top vegan food blog quarrygirl.com*

· ·

BABY 2$
SPiNach

Chapter 2 | Raw Basics

Preparing raw foods in your kitchen is not very different from cooking foods. Most of the ingredients are familiar, but instead of baking, frying, and sautéing, you'll be soaking, blending, processing, and dehydrating. It may seem strange at first, but with practice it will become second nature. This chapter will equip you with the culinary skills to successfully (and pleasurably) make everything in this book. And, keep in mind, your raw repertoire will grow and expand over time.

Stocking Your Pantry

Farmers' markets are one of your best bets for getting the freshest foods at the best price. Health food stores also offer a variety of produce as well as many of the spices and condiments on the following shopping list. If you can't find what you're looking for locally, check online for deals on raw food supplies, gadgets, and equipment. See "Resources" on page 189 for some of my favorite websites.

RAW GROCERY STORE GUIDE

Here are a few of the many staples I like to have on hand in my pantry; many are used regularly in this book. Use this as your shopping list, because you'll be able to make the majority of the recipes using just these ingredients.

Fruits: Look for fresh, unbruised fruit. I rarely buy frozen fruit, but if I have an excess I'll freeze or juice it so it doesn't go to waste.

* Lemons
* Limes
* Apples
* Oranges
* Bananas
* Avocados
* Young Thai coconuts
* And a little bit of whatever is currently in season

Vegetables: Avoid precut, prepackaged vegetables that have been sitting in plastic bags and containers for who knows how long. Instead, pick loose, vibrant-looking vegetables and buy only as much as you will use in five to seven days.

* Kale
* Spinach
* Romaine lettuce
* Cucumbers
* Celery
* Parsley
* Zucchini
* Onions (red, white, yellow)
* Tomatoes
* Bell peppers (red, orange, and yellow; not green—they're unripe!)

Herbs: Growing your own herbs is easy and economical. If you have more than you can use, just dry them in the dehydrator and store in jars for future use.

* Mint
* Basil
* Thyme
* Oregano
* Chives
* Rosemary

Raw nuts and seeds: Buy what you'll use within a month and store them in the refrigerator to maintain their freshness. Soak and dehydrate nuts immediately when you bring them home so they're ready to be used in raw recipes when you need them. See "Soaking Nuts and Seeds" on page 46.

* Brazil nuts
* Pecans
* Walnuts
* Cashews
* Almonds
* Pumpkin seeds
* Sunflower seeds
* Hemp seeds (do not need soaking)
* Flaxseeds (soak right before using)
* Chia seeds (soak right before using)

Grains: Buy what you'll use in a month and store in an airtight container.

* Oat groats
* Rolled oats
* Kamut
* Spelt
* Hulled buckwheat
* Hand parched wild rice

Nut and seed butters: You can find raw nut butters at most health food stores. Once opened, store in the refrigerator and use within two months.

* Almond butter
* Cashew butter
* Raw tahini

Oils: Look for organic, cold-pressed, extra-virgin oils to get the best flavor and highest nutrient content. Olive, flax, and sesame oils should be kept in the refrigerator and away from light. They go rancid quickly, so use them within one month. Coconut oil is very shelf stable and can last in your pantry for several weeks.

* Olive oil
* Flax oil
* Unrefined coconut oil
* Toasted sesame oil (not a raw food, but a nice thing to have when you want to add a "cooked" flavor to a dish)

Salts: Toss the chemically processed, iodized salt and instead use a trace mineral–rich, natural sea salt or pink salt. These are my three favorites.

* Celtic sea salt
* Himalayan pink salt
* Hawaiian sea salt

Condiments: These are not crucial to have, but they do bring a variety of great flavors to raw foods.

* Bragg apple cider vinegar
* Balsamic vinegar
* Nutritional yeast
* Nama shoyu or tamari (fermented, traditionally brewed soy sauces)
* Tamarind paste
* Sweet, white, or chickpea miso paste

Spices and flavorings: Purchase dried herbs in small quantities and replace them every six months.

- Fresh garlic
- Fresh ginger
- Vanilla beans
- Sun-dried tomatoes (dry, not packed in oil)
- Dried olives
- Dulse flakes
- Cacao powder and nibs
- Whole nutmeg
- Cinnamon sticks
- Garlic powder
- Onion powder
- Cayenne pepper
- Crushed red pepper
- Turmeric
- Pumpkin pie spice blend
- Italian seasoning blend
- Curry seasoning blend
- Peppercorns

Sun-dried fruits: When possible, use sun-dried fruits, because other dried fruits are factory dried at high temperatures. If sun dried is not available, it is perfectly acceptable to use whatever is available.

- Raisins
- Zante currants
- Dates
- Cranberries
- Goji berries
- Dried shredded coconut

Sweeteners: I use various sweeteners, depending on the recipe. My most used are agave nectar, palm sugar, and maple syrup.

- Agave nectar (clear)
- Palm sugar
- Maple syrup (grade B)
- Raw honey (liquid or cream)
- Evaporated cane juice (rapadura)
- Stevia (dried, powdered, or liquid)

FOOD STORAGE TIPS

- Avocados should be kept on the counter until ripe (they should give when you squeeze them). You can store ripe avocados in the refrigerator for several days.

- Tomatoes should be kept on the counter—never in the refrigerator.

- Bananas should be kept on the counter until they develop freckles. Peel and slice bananas when ripe and store in an airtight container or reclosable zippered plastic bag in the freezer for one month. It is best to use them within a week, before they start to brown.

- Garlic and onions should be stored in a cool, dry, dark place.

- Greens such as lettuce and fresh herbs should be stored in tightly sealed plastic bags or containers in the crisper section of your refrigerator. (I like to store all of my produce in Evert-Fresh Green Bags. They stay fresh much longer.)

RAW-ISH FOODS

Some ingredients in this book are not actually raw but are included because of their culinary usefulness and flavor. Except to the raw food purists, these are considered acceptable. Some of these are:

* **Cashews,** most conventional brands of which are steamed for removal from their toxic shells.

* **Rolled oats** are usually heated during processing. Some companies do offer truly raw oats.

* **Maple syrup,** which is boiled during production but is still rich in minerals and has an unbeatable flavor.

* **Miso paste,** which contains cooked beans, rice, and grains but also has beneficial bacteria, making it a "living food."

* **Wild rice,** which is heated during the drying process.

* Bragg apple cider **vinegar** is raw, though balsamic, rice, and other vinegars are not. They are acidic to the body, so I use them only occasionally to flavor foods.

* Almost all concentrated **sweeteners**. These have been processed to some degree. Raw honey, dates, and dried stevia leaf (not powder) are the only truly raw sweeteners, and possibly some brands of agave nectar.

The Agave Controversy

The use of agave nectar has been somewhat controversial. Some holistic health leaders have claimed that the fructose content does more harm than good, and there is debate as to how pure it is and whether it is raw or not. As with all concentrated sweeteners, try to use it only occasionally. Do your own research and determine for yourself whether agave nectar fits into your diet. If not, there are plenty of other sweeteners to experiment with. I have offered sweetener options in some of the recipes, but I have not tested most of them with alternative sweeteners.

The Tools

The first year I ate raw I had only a cheap kitchen knife and a low-end blender that came with a mini food processor attachment. I was able to make wonderful creations with what I had, but boy, have I come a long way since then. It is truly a joy to have great kitchen equipment, but if you don't have the tools yet, don't sweat it. Tons of great recipes out there require only a knife. In the beginning, I started a kitchen fund so every few weeks I could purchase one tool at a time until I had what I needed. I recommend you start with the knife, then the blender, then a food processor, and lastly the dehydrator, and watch your culinary world open up. Also, you don't have to buy everything new. High-end, high-horsepower blenders such as the Vita-Mix are like tanks: They last forever, so if your great aunt wants to give you hers, by all means take it! One student I had found all her kitchen tools on online classified ads. The Internet is the best place to search for the top deals on big-ticket items, while yard and garage sales are perfect places to stumble upon kitchen gadgets.

CHEF'S KNIFE

Having a good-quality chef's knife makes all the difference in the world. Splurge on a good one and it will become your best friend in the kitchen. Look for one with a 6- to 8-inch (15- to 20-cm) nonserrated blade. Ceramic knives are becoming increasingly popular because of their light weight and their ability to stay sharp for years. Raw foodists use them because they don't oxidize food the way metal does. Unfortunately, they can break easily, so they are not appropriate for opening coconuts or cutting anything too hard or fibrous.

BLENDER

A high-speed blender is no ordinary blender. These powerhouses are found in every profes-
sional kitchen and restaurant and can make the silkiest sauces, smoothies, soups, and creams
you've ever had. There are two popular high-speed blenders on the market: the Vita-Mix and
the Blendtec. The Vita-Mix can go from very low speed to turbo and has a 64-ounce (1,792 ml)
container for big recipes and a 32-ounce (896 ml) container for whipping up smaller batches (sold
separately). The Blendtec has preprogrammed sequences you can choose depending on whether
you're making a smoothie or a soup or crushing ice and will automatically stop when the processing is complete. The Vita-Mix is like driving a stick shift while the Blendtec is like driving an auto-
matic. Both are great; it just depends on what you like. High-speed blenders will run you a pretty
penny, but they are a great investment if you have any sort of culinary passion. If a fancy blender
doesn't fit your budget right now, don't be discouraged. Many of the recipes in this book will work
just fine in an average household blender. It will just take a little more time to get a smoother consistency for some of the recipes. If high-speed power is essential to the recipe, I will specifically say
to use a high-power blender; otherwise, you may use a household blender.

Blending Tips:

* Always put wet ingredients into the container first, followed by dry ingredients to allow the
  blades to move more easily.

* The friction from blending too long can heat up your food and actually cook it. Pay attention if
  you're blending for longer than two minutes.

* Always keep the lid on the container and never walk away while it is blending. I learned that
  lesson the hard way.

FOOD PROCESSOR

Food processors are better suited for solid foods, while blenders are better suited for working
with liquids. Food processors use different kinds of blades, but the one most often used is the
"S" blade. Named for its shape, it's most useful for chopping and homogenizing. Occasionally, a
recipe may call for shredded ingredients, for which you can use the shredding plate if you have
one. It's extremely quick and will save you a bit a time, especially if you're shredding several heads
of cabbage to make sauerkraut (see page 164). For this book, always use the "S" blade unless
otherwise specified. Also, I recommend at least a 7-cup (1,645 ml) food processor for the recipes
in this book. Nowadays many food processors come with a large and a small container. My current
one has a 12-cup (2,820 ml) and a 4-cup (940 ml) container and is perfect for all of my food-
processing needs.

Food Processing Tips:

* Use the Pulse button when you want to chop something into small pieces, such as tomatoes for
  salsa. Use the On button when you want to homogenize.

* Be careful when handling the blades, because they can be extremely sharp.

DEHYDRATOR

Excalibur dehydrators are the raw foodist's version of ovens. They have a temperature control dial so your food is not overheated and are well designed for making breads, crackers, chips, tortillas, granola, fruit leathers, and other snacks. They can also be used to warm your food, speed the marinating of vegetables, thicken sauces, and soften coconut butter. Excalibur dehydrators are best suited for making raw foods, though other brands may be more available in other markets. If you get a different brand, just make sure it has a temperature control dial, and do consumer research on any model you consider buying.

Drying Tips:

* Always dehydrate food below 118°F (48°C) to preserve the enzymes and thus its healthful properties.

* Occasionally, a recipe will instruct you to start at 145°F (63°C) for one hour and then lower to 110°F (46°C). This helps evaporate water more quickly, thereby minimizing the chance of mold growth. This method has been rigorously tested, and it is proven that the food's temperature does not go over 118°F (48°C) when the temperature is at 145°F (63°C) if left for one hour or less.

Using a Dehydrator

The Excalibur dehydrators have large square trays lined with removable mesh screens. When we want to dry foods such as a purée or foods that contain a lot of moisture, like when making flax crackers, a nonstick sheet is placed over the mesh screen. These are also called Teflex or ParaFlexx sheets and can be purchased through Excalibur. You can also use parchment paper, but the drying times will vary and the foods usually take longer to dry.

In some of the recipes I will instruct you to transfer items from the nonstick sheets onto the mesh screens so that the food dries evenly. To do this:

1. Place another tray with the mesh screen over the tray you are using (a & b).
2. Hold both sides of the trays tightly together and flip (c).
3. Remove the top tray and peel away the nonstick sheet (d).
4. Continue to dry as instructed.

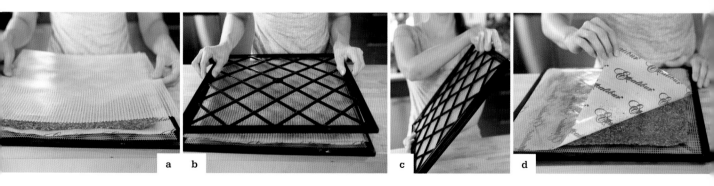

a   b   c   d

Other Tips:

* Because the fan is in the back of the unit, I like to rotate my trays every few hours from front to back to ensure even drying.

* Drying times are not a perfect science. Water content can vary each time you make a particular recipe, so be prepared for it take an hour or so longer or shorter. This can also happen if you have other foods in the dehydrator at the same time.

* Remove any trays that are not in use to increase the airflow.

JUICER

Juicers are an important part of a raw food diet. Drinking juice is a great way to give our digestive system a rest while still acquiring enzymes, vitamins, and minerals. Fasting on juice is very therapeutic and is used for cleansing and for healing many illnesses. There are two basic types of juicers.

* **Centrifugal juicers** chop and masticate the fruit or vegetable and spin them in a plastic or steel basket at high speed, separating the pulp from the juice. The high-speed spinning oxidizes the juice, thereby losing some of the nutrients. Be aware that not all centrifugal juicers can handle green leaves or wheatgrass.

* **Masticating juicers** slowly grind the fruit and vegetables into a paste and then squeeze the juice through a screen at the bottom. I prefer to use masticating juicers because there is less oxidation and I can juice everything from green leafy vegetables and wheatgrass to root vegetables, as well as create nut butters and banana soft-serve ice cream.

Juicing Tips:

* It's best to drink fresh juice as soon as you make it. Masticated juice will keep in an airtight jar for up to 24 hours. After that, much of its vitality is lost.
* Chew your juice to activate saliva and digestive enzymes.
* Green vegetable juice can remineralize your teeth, so swish it around before you swallow.
* The juice pulp can be used for other food preparations or used for compost.

* * *

Raw food was a journey into self ... It gave me new eyes with which to see. I rediscovered a depth of being that has forever transformed my life. There are no rules, only choices ... and self-love is the number-one ingredient in optimal nutrition.

—*Gabrielle Brick, health motivator and longevity specialist*
www.gabriellebrick.com

Basic Knife Skills

A great chef's knife and a large wooden or bamboo cutting board will make slicing and dicing easy, safe, and enjoyable. Here are some basic cutting terms and simple instructions used in this book.

CHOP

When chopping food, try to make pieces uniform in size and shape (top left).

MINCE

Mincing is a very fine chop usually called for when preparing herbs and/or garlic. Hold the end of the knife steady while moving it in a fanning motion to chop (top right).

JULIENNE

This is a technique used to create long, rectangular "matchstick" shapes.

TO JULIENNE A BELL PEPPER:

1. Slice 1 inch (2.5 cm) from the top of the pepper all the way around but not through to the core (a)
2. Remove the top section and pull out the seeds (b).
3. Cut the bottom of the pepper (c) and make a slice down the middle (d).
4. Lay the pepper flat and slice off any remaining core pieces (e).
5. Slice the pepper into equal-size matchsticks (f).

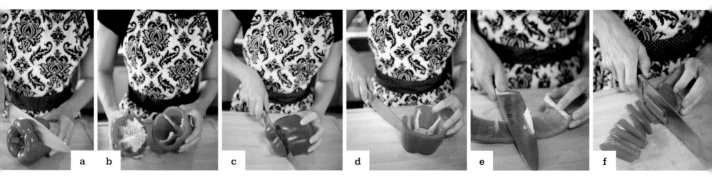

a   b   c   d   e   f

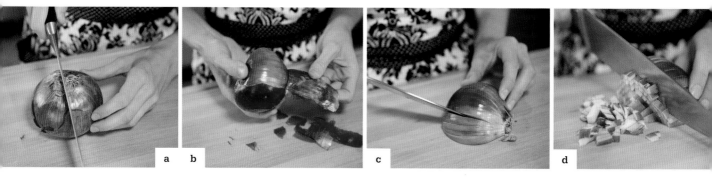

DICE

This technique is used to create a cube shape.

TO DICE AN ONION:
1. Slice an onion in half lengthwise (through the root) (a) and remove the outer skin (b).
2. Slice along the natural lines of the onion (c).
3. Slice crosswise to create a dice (d).

TO DICE A BELL PEPPER (NOT SHOWN):
1. Group several julienned pieces together and cut crosswise into equal-size cubes.

CHIFFONADE

This is a simple way to turn leafy greens and herbs into elegant ribbons.

1. Stack a few leaves evenly on your cutting board (a).
2. Use your fingers to grasp the edges nearest you and roll the leaves into a tight cigar shape (b).
3. Thinly slice your rolled leaves. Curl your fingers (c) so you don't accidentally slice them too!
4. Use the ribbons to garnish soups, salads, and entrées (d).

DESTEM KALE

With one hand, hold the end of the stem (a) while the other hand quickly pushes the kale leaves down along the stem and off (b & c).

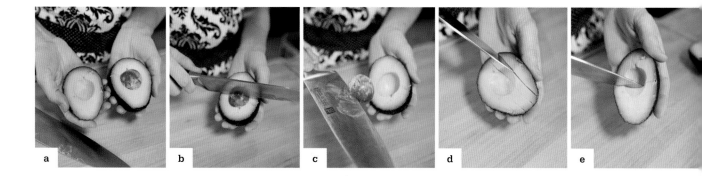

SLICE AND DICE AN AVOCADO

1. Slice the avocado lengthwise all the way around and pull it apart (a).
2. With a short quick motion, hit the avocado pit with the edge of the knife. Place the avocado on the countertop instead of holding it in your hands until you get the hang of it (b).
3. Twist the knife to remove the pit (c).
4. Make lengthwise cuts to make slices (d).
5. Make crosswise cuts to dice, and scoop out with a spoon (e).

Using a Mandoline

A mandoline, such as the one pictured above, is not a essential tool, but it's great for creating sliced and julienned vegetables and fruit. Dozens of different types of mandolines are on the market, but in my kitchen I have two that I use daily. They're simple and convenient to use, and best of all, easy to clean.

CERAMIC MANDOLINE

These are very lightweight and have a double-edged ceramic blade. They create paper-thin slices, which I love for preparing onions and shallots for my salads. The blade is sharp yet safer than other types of mandolines.

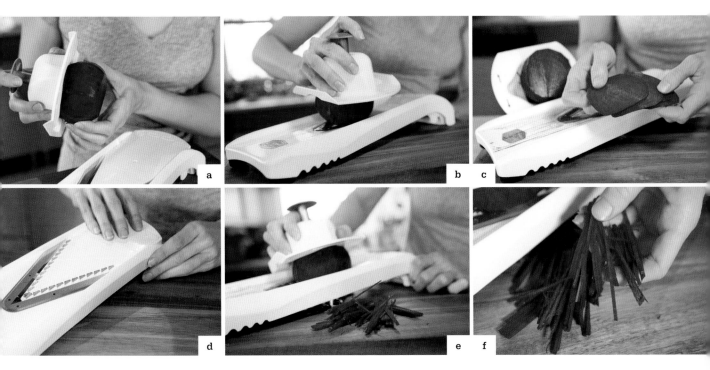

V SLICER

The V slicer is lightweight and comes with three different slicing inserts. It makes
$\frac{1}{16}$-inch (1.5 mm) and ¼-inch (6 mm) slices and can also julienne your vegetables.

I recommend using the hand guard or a protective glove when cutting smaller vegetables on the V
slicer, because the blade is extremely sharp and will get you when you're not paying attention. It is
very simple to use and is a great time-saver.

1. To use, attach the food holder/hand guard firmly (a).
2. Use quick downward strokes into the blade (b).
3. You can create uniform slices (c).
4. You can julienne your vegetables using the shredder insert (d, e, & f).

a   b   c

SPIRAL VEGETABLE SLICER

These handy gadgets allow you to turn your vegetables into versatile noodles. They are becoming increasingly popular, and a basic one costs only about twenty to forty dollars. Every model is slightly different, but most will turn your zucchini, cucumbers, daikon radish, and carrots into fun spaghetti and ribbon noodles.

The best vegetables to spiralize are ones that are thick and straight and don't contain too many seeds that can clog the blades.

FOR ZUCCHINI NOODLES:

1. Slice both ends of the zucchini crosswise.
2. Insert one end into the center of the cutting blade (a) and secure the other end with the prongs (b).
3. Push the zucchini toward the blade gently while simultaneously rotating the crank (c).

KITCHEN GADGET CHECKLIST

* Paring knife
* Knife sharpener
* Cutting board
* Measuring cups
* Measuring spoons
* Nut milk bag
* Citrus reamer/juicer
* Vegetable spiralizer
* Bash and chop
* Spice grinder

* Rubber spatula
* Kitchen scissors
* Mixing bowls
* Vegetable peeler
* Garlic press
* Pepper grinder
* Offset spatula
* Squeeze bottles
* Colander/strainer

* Half-gallon (2 L), 1-quart (946 ml), and half-pint (235 ml) wide-mouthed mason jars
* Hand shredder/grater
* Cutting board scraper
* Salad spinner
* Bamboo sushi mat
* Fine zester/grater (microplane)
* Storage containers

Raw Techniques

USING COCONUTS

Two popular types of coconuts are available at most health food stores and Asian markets: the iconic, fuzzy brown coconuts and young Thai coconuts. Young Thai coconuts are white, husked coconuts with cut, cone-shaped tops and are usually sold wrapped in plastic, in the refrigerated produce section.

Mature coconuts have very thick, dry meat and little water, while young coconuts have a small amount of soft meat and contain 1 to 1½ cups (235 to 355 ml) of water. Look for ones with a soft, spongy husk and no dark, purple spots or cracks on the bottom. Only young Thai coconuts are used for the recipes in this book.

Coconut water is very high in potassium and other electrolytes and is a great alternative to sugary sports drinks. You can add it to smoothies or blend it with a handful of spinach to make a sweet and frothy work-out recovery drink. Coconut meat will last for three days in the refrigerator or indefinitely in the freezer.

HEALTH BENEFITS OF COCONUTS

Coconuts have a long list of health benefits, thanks to the presence of lauric acid, a precursor to monolaurin that acts as an antimicrobial, antioxidant, antifungal, and antibacterial agent. Coconut oil in particular is excellent for skin conditions such as dermatitis, eczema, and psoriasis when taken internally as well as applied externally on problem areas.

Coconut oil:

* Is helpful in killing viruses that cause influenza, herpes, hepatitis, and measles
* Is helpful in killing bacteria that cause ulcers, gum disease, and throat infections
* Is helpful in killing fungi and yeasts that cause candidiasis, ringworm, and athlete's foot
* Reduces the production of LDL, "bad" cholesterol
* Is rapidly burned by the liver in the form of glucose
* Increases metabolism
* Boosts the immune system
* Reduces inflammation and aids in tissue repair
* Improves digestion and the absorption of vitamins and minerals

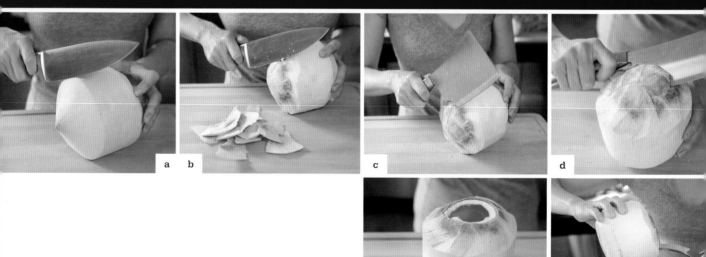

a b   c   d

e   f

MATERIALS
Sharp knife
Cleaver
Fine-mesh strainer
Large bowl
Rubber (or silicone) spatula
Paring knife

NOTE: Make sure your knife and cleaver are very sharp, and be extremely cautious when handling them!

Opening the Coconut

1. Use a sharp knife to remove the husk from the top portion or "cone" of the coconut, exposing the brown nut (a & b).

2. Turn the coconut on its side and hold firmly from the bottom. With the heel of a sharp cleaver, aim for the outermost part of the exposed nut and give it a firm whack (c). It may take a few tries, depending on the coconut. *Note: Stay focused when using a cleaver. Do not raise your arm above your head or expose your fingers anywhere near the target.*

3. Once you have the heel firmly in the nut, turn the coconut on its base and lift the cleaver to create a flap (d & e). This will happen naturally—the crack will always create a perfect circle.

4. Pour the coconut water through a fine strainer before using to remove any shell pieces (f).

5. The water should be clear or slightly cloudy and sweet. If it is purple, pink, or cloudy, or if it smells off, you should discard the entire coconut. Always do a taste test before using coconut water in a recipe. Store the coconut water in the refrigerator and use it within three days.

Scraping Coconut Meat

1. Use a rubber spatula to scrape out the meat (g & h). Depending on how young the coconut is, you will have meat ranging from very gelatinous to thick and firm.

2. Remove any bits of shell with a paring knife (i).

3. Slice the meat with a sharp knife (j).

Firm coconut meat is great for making into noodles and coconut jerky, while the softer meat is great for sauces and smoothies.

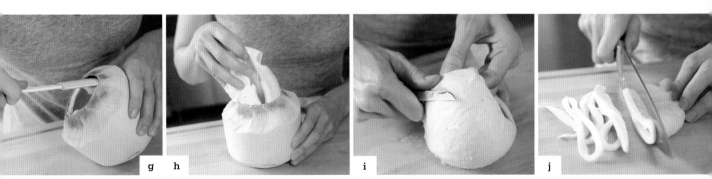

g   h   i   j

MATERIALS

Yield: about 4 cups (660 g)

**1-quart (946 ml) glass jar
with lid**

¾ cup (120 g) wild rice

Filtered water

BLOOMING WILD RICE

Wild rice doesn't actually sprout, so I like to use the term "bloom" to describe the process of softening and splitting the rice. Wild rice is not actually rice but a marsh grass seed that grows in North America, predominantly in the Great Lakes region. It's technically not raw but is still used in raw dishes because it is highly nutritious and very satisfying. It has a wonderful nutty flavor and is a great transition food if you're new to raw. It has no gluten and is high in protein, especially the amino acid lysine, as well as high in fiber and a great source of potassium, phosphorus, and B vitamins. The best wild rice to use in raw food recipes is hand-parched wild lake rice from Wilderness Family Naturals. Most store-bought wild rice is hybridized or not processed in a way that yields good results.

TO BLOOM RICE:

1. Put ¾ cup (120 g) rice into a 1-quart (946 ml) mason jar and fill to the top with filtered water (a).
2. Secure the lid and place in a dehydrator for 12 to 24 hours at 110°F (46°C) (b).
3. Remove the jar from the dehydrator. Pour the rice through a strainer and rinse well (c).

Your rice is now ready to use. Store in the refrigerator for up to one week in a water-filled jar. Change the water daily to maintain freshness.

a   b   c

SPICES AND HERBS: TRADITIONAL HEALING IN OUR PANTRY

Spices and herbs are not just for bringing great flavor to recipes. For centuries they were used for their healing properties. Here are some of the familiar ones that bring wonderful taste and wellness to our plates.

* **Allspice:** increases circulation; aids indigestion and gas

* **Anise:** aids cough and other respiratory problems by breaking up mucus; helps increase milk production for nursing mothers

* **Basil:** good for indigestion, fevers, colds, flus, headaches, nausea, vomiting, and cramps

* **Black pepper:** improves digestion by stimulating hydrochloric acid production in the stomach; stimulates the breakdown of fat cells

* **Cardamom:** good for headaches, indigestion, and gas; warms the body

* **Cayenne:** good for circulation; helps prevent heart attacks, strokes, colds, flu, headaches, indigestion, and arthritis

* **Cinnamon:** warms the system; balances blood sugar levels; treats diarrhea, cramps, abdominal pains, coughing, wheezing, and lower back pain

* **Clove:** increases circulation; improves digestion; treats vomiting and nausea; oil of cloves can relieve toothaches

* **Cumin:** prevents and relieves indigestion, gas, nausea, and morning sickness; helps relieve cold symptoms

* **Dill:** useful for abdominal pains and cramps, indigestion, colds, flus, and coughs

* **Fennel:** helps treat colic, cramps, and gas; expels mucus

* **Garlic:** supports the immune system; helps eliminate parasites and infections; aids high and low blood pressure, lung ailments, and headaches

* **Ginger:** good for circulation and warmth, indigestion, cramps, and nausea

* **Lavender:** antidepressant; helps relieve headaches, anxiety, and insomnia

* **Mint:** aids digestion; the aroma eases nausea, headaches, and respiratory disorders

* **Nutmeg:** can help relieve nervous disorders and heart problems

* **Oregano:** contains very strong antibacterial properties and antioxidant activities

* **Paprika:** increases saliva production, which aids digestion; helps regulate blood pressure; improves circulation

* **Rosemary:** helps treat headaches, indigestion, colic, nausea, gas, and fevers

* **Sage:** useful for diarrhea and early stages of cold, flu, and sinus congestion; useful for bladder infections

* **Tarragon:** relieves stomach cramps and promotes appetite; aids digestion by increasing bile production in the liver

* **Thyme:** useful for eliminating intestinal worms, bronchial problems, chronic gastritis, and lack of appetite

* **Turmeric:** a blood purifier; helps circulation; regulates menstrual cycle; reduces fevers; powerful antioxidant with anticancer properties

* **Watercress:** blood cleanser; has anticancer properties; aids in eye health; increases digestive juices

* **Yellow mustard:** aids respiratory and kidney problems; helps protect against gastrointestinal cancer

MATERIALS
Cutting board
Paring knife
Spice grinder (optional)

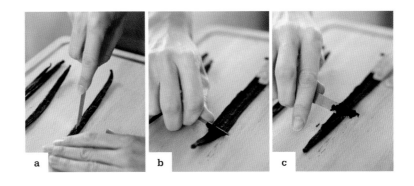

a   b   c

OPENING A VANILLA BEAN

Aromatic, fresh vanilla beans are wonderful additions to desserts and nut milks. Buy them inexpensively in bulk so you always have some on hand. (See "Resources" on page 189 for bulk sources.)

1. Using a paring knife, carefully make a slit down the center of the bean without slicing all the way through (a).
2. Open the bean and scrape the seeds out with the knife (b & c). Scraped beans can be ground with a spice grinder to use in desserts. You can steep whole beans in herbal teas as well.

SOAKING NUTS AND SEEDS

Mother Nature created some raw nuts and seeds to contain enzyme inhibitors that keep them dormant and from spontaneously growing. Soaking nuts is important because it makes them easier to blend, but it also removes these enzyme inhibitors. Removing them decreases some of the acidity and bitterness and makes them easier to digest.

SOAK TIMES FOR NUTS AND SEEDS

Almonds	8–12 hours	Pecans	2–4 hours
Brazil nuts	2 hours	Pumpkin seeds	4–6 hours
Buckwheat	6–8 hours	Rye berries	10 hours
Cashews	2 hours	Sesame seeds	4–6 hours
Chia	6–8 hours	Sunflower seeds	4–6 hours
Flax	4–6 hours	Walnuts	6–8 hours
Hazelnuts	2 hours	Wheat berries	10 hours
Hemp seeds	Not necessary to soak		

Not all nuts need to be soaked. For example, cashews, Brazil nuts, and macadamia nuts do not contain enzyme inhibitors but may require soaking to make them easier to blend in certain recipes. Be careful not to oversoak, because essential minerals can start to leach into the soak water.

To soak, place nuts in a bowl and cover with plenty of filtered water so they can absorb and expand.

Always rinse the nuts and seeds well before using them. You can store soaked nuts and seeds in the refrigerator for several days or dry them at 110°F (46°C) for 8 to 12 hours or until crisp and store them in an airtight container. Chia and flaxseeds will absorb soak water and become gelatinous. I only soak them just before I'm ready to use them.

· ✳ ·

Note: Pasteurized almonds can still be labeled as raw even though they do not have the vitality of a truly raw almond. Luckily, truly raw almonds can be purchased directly from the farmers. See "Resources" on page 189 for where you can order them online.

· ·

SPROUTS

Sprouts are considered the ultimate living food. Small and mighty, these little guys pack a nutritional punch, even more so than in their mature, adult stage. One ounce (28 g) of broccoli sprouts contains the same antioxidant quantity as three heads of broccoli and has been shown to be a beneficial part of some cancer treatments. Growing your own sprouts is not only economical, but they also taste much better and fresher than store-bought sprouts. There are a few different methods, but here are the two that I use in my kitchen.

Jar Method

Many websites sell glass jars with specially fitted caps that allow airflow. You could grow sprouts using any size jar you have at home, but I recommend getting at least a couple of wide-mouth 1-quart (946 ml) jars, or if you have a bigger household, a couple of half-gallon (2 L) jars. By having multiple jars going at different times you will always have fresh sprouts to add to your salads and juices. You can substitute the fitted cap with window-screen material from a hardware store and secure it with a rubber band.

Some popular and tasty sprouts that do well with the jar method are alfalfa, clover, broccoli, radish, onion, and arugula.

1. Soak 2 tablespoons (18 g) of seeds per quart (L) filled two-thirds of the way with room-temperature (65° to 75°F [18° to 24°C]) water (a). Soak 3 to 8 hours for alfalfa and clover, 8 hours or overnight for other seeds. The harder and larger the seed, the longer it should soak.
2. Pour out the soak water (b) (great for houseplants!) and rinse the sprouts well with room-temperature (65° to 75°F [18° to 24°C]) water. Cold water will shock your sprouts and inhibit growth, while hot water will either kill your sprouts or promote mold growth.

3. Place the jar in a shady area at a 45-degree angle (a dish rack works well) and make sure the seeds are not all gathered at the opening (c). There should be plenty of space for air to circulate.

4. Rinse and drain the seeds two or three times a day, depending on the temperature. Rinse more often in warmer environments.

5. On the fourth or fifth day your sprouts will be ready to go (d). You may leave them near a sunny window for a day to develop chlorophyll.

6. Rinse a final time and put the sprouts in a large mixing bowl filled with cool water (e).

7. Detangle and move the sprouts around so the hulls float to the surface and gently move them to the sides of the bowl (f).

8. Remove the sprouts from the bowl and let sit in a colander (g) or lay on a clean towel to dry. You may eat them immediately; otherwise, allow them to completely dry before storing.

9. Wrap the sprouts in paper towels and place in a tightly closed Evert-Fresh bag and keep in the crisper of your refrigerator. You may also use a dry glass jar (the one you used to sprout in). Don't store wet sprouts in the refrigerator or they will mold.

a   b   c   d

e   f g

Tray Method

This is a good method for growing sunflower sprouts and wheatgrass. You will need seeds, water, two cafeteria trays, and organic potting soil.

FOR SUNFLOWER SEEDS:

1. Soak your seeds for 8 to 14 hours in a sprouting jar. Seeds will float, so fill completely to the top with water. Use ⅔ cup (97 g) of seeds for a 10 x 14-inch (25 x 36-cm) tray or 1 cup (145 g) of seeds for a 14 x 16-inch (36 x 40-cm) tray.
2. Drain and rinse and then store in a shady spot at a 45-degree angle.
3. Rinse at least twice a day just until rootlets begin to emerge (1 to 2 days). Transfer before they grow longer than ¼ inch (6 mm).
4. Fill a tray with ¾ to 1 inch (2 to 2.5 cm) of potting soil (a) and spread seeds evenly so that each one has contact with the soil (b).
5. Add enough water so the soil is moist but not soaked (c). You can drain excess water by tilting the tray over the sink. Too much water will create mold, but too little will kill your seeds.
6. Cover with a second tray (d).
7. Mist with water as necessary to keep soil and seeds moist one or two times a day. On the third day the seedlings will begin to lift the tray up (e). When it has lifted ½ inch (1.3 cm), remove the tray and move the sprouts to a partly sunny window.
8. By the sixth or seventh day your sprouts are ready to harvest. Shake the shell fragments gently off (f) and cut sprouts just above the soil line with scissors (g). *Note*: Don't water your sprouts for 12 hours before harvesting. They will stay crisper during storage if they are dry.

Store the sprouts wrapped in a paper towel in a tightly sealed Evert-Fresh green bag or an airtight container and keep in the refrigerator for about 1 week.

For more information about growing sprouts I recommend a book called *Sprout Garden* by Mark Mathew Braunstein.

NOTE ON SPROUTING GRAINS

To sprout grains (shown here is kamut), soak 1¾ cups (326 g) of seeds in purified water for 8 to 12 hours in a 1-quart (946-ml) glass sprouting jar. Rinse well and then store the jar at a 45-degree angle for 12 to 24 hours, away from direct sunlight, rinsing at least twice a day. Sprouted grains are best when rootlets are ¼ inch (6 mm) long or as long as the seed. Alternatively, you can soak seeds in a bowl and then allow them to sprout in a large strainer or colander, covered loosely with a tea towel. Rinse twice a day. Sprouted seeds will yield 4 cups (660 g).

d

e

f

g

Think like a Chef

When I started making raw foods I was no domestic goddess in the kitchen. Things such as soaking, sprouting, and dehydrating were completely foreign to me—but blending? That I could do, so I started there. Find the recipes that fit your experience level and dive in. Don't be afraid to try new things, though. The more you do it, the faster and easier it will be next time.

FOOD SUBSTITUTIONS

You might find a recipe you really want to try, but you may not have all of the ingredients available. Or maybe a recipe contains more fat, sugar, or salt than you would like. Most raw recipes are versatile and very forgiving if you need to reduce, substitute, or omit ingredients.

FOR EXAMPLE:

* If you want to reduce the sodium in a savory salad, use dulse flakes instead of sea salt. Just keep in mind that dulse has a bit of an ocean flavor.

* Lemons can be used instead of vinegars in salad dressings and sauces.

* Limes can be replaced with lemons.

* Dates can be used in place of agave. Use two Medjool dates for each tablespoon (15 ml) of agave nectar. Additional water may be needed, depending on the recipe.

* Cashews can be replaced with almonds, macadamias, or pine nuts in sauces and creams.

* Maple syrup, honey, and agave nectar are interchangeable, though agave has a neutral flavor and is less sweet.

* Pears can be replaced with apples and vice versa.

* Seaweeds, except for Irish moss, are easy to exchange for each other, but read the instructions on the package. Some need to be soaked and rinsed before using, and some do not.

If, during your transition from eating cooked foods to raw foods, you feel the need for some hot foods, you can heat many of these recipes on a stovetop or in the oven at low (warm) temperature. You'll lose some nutrients, but you'll still have a healthy meal. You can also substitute some of the raw wraps with sprouted tortillas or bread. Spaghetti Bolognese and Creamy Tomato Fettuccine can be served over cooked rice noodles with some zucchini noodles mixed in.

Also, don't be afraid to experiment. I've given variations and suggestions in many of the recipes, but I'm sure you can come up with plenty of your own that suit your tastes.

Chapter 3

Recipes for the Revolution

WE'VE COME A LONG WAY SINCE THE 1970's and its bland, boring version of the raw food diet: carrot sticks and simple salads. Most people new to eating raw are surprised to discover how flavorful and satisfying it is. Today, we have access to versatile and unique ingredients such as young Thai coconuts and raw cacao, which make stunning desserts that rival their cooked counterparts. Newly developed culinary techniques turn raw ingredients into tantalizing, gourmet creations while retaining maximum nutrition.

Though we need food for nourishment, we also need food to taste exquisite and be pleasing to the eye. Are not the most memorable meals the ones where every human sense is enticed? Don't be discouraged if you've never been proficient in the kitchen. Balancing flavor, creating texture, and beautiful presentation are culinary arts that anyone can master. With raw foods, there are countless possibilities within the parameters of not heating them. Sometimes you just have to think outside the box. As you read through the recipes, I hope you are inspired. These are all recipes for you to take and run with. Add your own twist to them. Experiment with different ingredients and don't be afraid to make mistakes—that is how the best recipes are born.

The following chapter is a collection of raw favorites from my kitchen that are bold and light, with a few indulgent dishes for when we crave some comfort food.

Smoothies

It's a fact that in the morning, our digestive system takes just as much time to wake up as the rest of our body does. The best way to gently get it going is by drinking easy-to-digest juices and smoothies. They're hydrating and packed with nutrients to replenish vitamins and minerals lost during the night and provide energy without feeling weighed down. Oftentimes, starting the day on a healthy note continues throughout the day—cravings are calmed when our body has all the nourishment it needs. I often start the day with a green juice and then move on to a smoothie a couple of hours later. Try replacing your regular breakfast with a juice and smoothie and see if your energy soars!

Sunshine Smoothie

Makes 2 servings
Prep time: 10 minutes
Soak time: 20 minutes

This sweet and tangy smoothie is packed with immune-boosting vitamin C. I included whole oranges instead of just the juice for the extra fiber and phytonutrients, but you can substitute 1 cup (235 ml) orange juice if you prefer a smoother texture.

¼ cup (30 g) goji berries, soaked 20 minutes

4 oranges, peeled, seeded, and chopped

1 cup (150 g) sliced frozen bananas

⅔ cup (160 ml) Basic Nut Milk (see page 160)

2 teaspoons camu camu powder

Place all ingredients in a blender and process until smooth. Give the blender a little extra time to purée the pith from the orange completely.

NUTRITION NOTE: Camu camu is a fruit from the Amazonian rain forest that contains more vitamin C than any other known plant. It is becoming increasingly popular in health food stores and can easily be purchased online. Some nutritionists say it has mood-balancing properties in addition to helping maintain healthy skin, hair, and gums.

Piña Colada Smoothie

Makes 2 servings
Prep time: 10 minutes

This light and creamy tropical delight is the innocent version of the official drink of Puerto Rico. If you're not strictly raw, no one has to know if it's not virgin!

1 cup (235 ml) young Thai coconut water

½ cup (40 g) young Thai coconut meat

2 cups (330 g) pineapple chunks

½ cup (120 g) ice

Process all ingredients in a high-power blender until smooth.

Mint Chocolate Chip Smoothie

Makes 2 servings
Prep time: 5 minutes

This low-fat smoothie is a delicious way to start the day or enjoy as a cool dessert on a warm day.

2 cups (475 ml) Basic Nut Milk (see page 160)

2 cups (300 g) sliced frozen bananas

2 tablespoons (22 g) cacao nibs, plus extra for garnish

2 tablespoons (12 g) chopped fresh mint, plus extra leaves for garnish

½ vanilla bean, scraped, or 1 teaspoon vanilla extract

Pinch of sea salt (optional)

Process all ingredients in high-power blender until smooth. Garnish with mint leaves and cacao nibs.

The IronMan/
IronMama Smoothie

Makes 2 servings
Prep time: 10 minutes
Soak time: 20 minutes

It isn't the best-looking kid on the block, but at 15 grams of protein per serving, this tasty smoothie will give you the endurance and nutrients your workout needs. It is also an excellent smoothie for the mother-to-be who needs that extra boost of good-quality protein, essential fatty acids, calcium, iron, and folic acid.

¼ cup (30 g) goji berries, soaked 20 minutes

2 bananas

1 cup (145 g) strawberries

1 cup (145 g) blueberries

2 cups (60 g) kale

3 tablespoons (54 g) hemp protein powder (I use Navitas Naturals)

2 tablespoons (30 g) bee pollen

1 tablespoon (15 g) tahini paste

1 tablespoon (15 ml) flax oil

2 teaspoons maca powder

1½ cups (355 ml) water

Place all ingredients in a blender and process until smooth. Serve immediately.

Chef's Tip: For a cold smoothie, use frozen fruit.

RAW TIPS FROM ANDREA CROSSMAN, HOLISTIC DOULA

What raw foods are great for expecting mothers and why?

Fresh raw fruits and vegetables are wonderfully nourishing and healing for all of us, including mamas-to-be. One category of foods I recommend in particular is high–water content foods. Pregnant women need to be diligent about staying hydrated, and foods like cucumber (95% water), watermelon (92% water), and lettuce (95% water) can be great for that.

Any warnings about raw foods?

Of course pregnant women need to avoid raw meat, fish, and soft cheeses. Conversely, raw fruits and vegetables are fantastic pregnancy foods—just make sure to wash them well, especially if buying conventional produce.

Is it okay for expecting mothers to go entirely raw?

If someone is already successful and feeling great on an entirely raw diet, she could certainly stay on it. Anyone, pregnant or not, on a raw, vegan, or even vegetarian diet should supplement with vitamin B_{12}. Adding more raw fruits, vegetables, nuts, and seeds will definitely provide a great nutritional boost for mama and baby. I don't recommend making huge dietary or activity changes once pregnant, but seemingly small changes can have huge impact. Swapping out a typical breakfast for a green smoothie and making sure to get 5 or more servings of raw fruits and veggies would be wonderful for anyone!

—*Andrea Crossman, BA, BS, Holistic RN*

Green Smoothies

Victoria Boutenko, a longtime raw foodist, educator, and author, was the one to really push green smoothies into the forefront of raw nutrition. Her books *Green for Life* and *Green Smoothie Revolution* explain how, by blending our greens, we can truly utilize all that green leafy vegetables have to offer. The chlorophyll, minerals, and protein content are easily assimilated and used by our body, as opposed to only 30 percent of it being usable if we chew greens with our teeth.

GREEN BANANAS

3 cups (450 g) sliced bananas

2 cups (110 g) chopped kale

1 cup (235 ml) coconut water

PEACHES & GREENS

3 cups (510 g) chopped peaches

2 cups (60 g) chopped spinach

1 cup (150 g) sliced bananas

1 cup (235 ml) Basic Nut Milk
(see page 160)

SMOOTH PEAR

3 ripe pears, chopped

½ cup (30 g) chopped parsley

1 cup (235 ml) water

1 tablespoon (15 ml) lemon juice

BLUEBERRY CREAM

2 cups (290 g) blueberries

1 cup (150 g) sliced bananas

2 cups (110 g) chopped Swiss
chard

1 cup (235 ml) Basic Nut Milk
(see page 160)

ENZYME TIME

1½ cups (250 g) pineapple
chunks

1½ cups (210 g) papaya chunks

2 cups (60 g) chopped spinach

1 cup (235 ml) coconut water

SAVORY SMOOTHIE

3 Roma tomatoes

2 cups (60 g) chopped spinach

1 clove garlic

1 cup (235 ml) water

Dash of cayenne pepper

Green smoothies are made of fruit, green leaves, and water. You can also use coconut water or nut milk in place of water.

Ideally you want to go for:

- 60 percent fruit (bananas, pineapple, papaya, mango, berries, acai)

- 40 percent green leaves (spinach, romaine, kale, collard, Swiss chard, dandelion)

- Water to thin

When first starting out use mild greens such as spinach and green leaf lettuce. Kale, collards, and Swiss chard have a stronger flavor, so use a little less until you get used to it.

Boost the nutritional content of your smoothies by adding superfoods such as hemp protein, bee pollen, maca, and spirulina. A tablespoon of coconut oil, flax oil, or tahini paste is nice, too, and will keep you feeling full longer.

You can also add avocados, nuts, and seeds to your smoothie to make it creamier. Soak nuts and seeds first to help them blend easier.

Chef's Tip: Add blueberries if your kids (or spouse) are afraid of the green color.

Listed here are a few of my favorites. I like keeping it simple, but you can use a variety of different fruits and greens in one smoothie. Be adventurous. Sky's the limit! These recipes yield about 1 large or 2 small servings. Just place all ingredients into a blender and process until smooth.

Juices

Juicing is a great way to give your digestive system a rest while still receiving plenty of nutrients. I often juice one day a week and do three- to seven-day fasts several times a year to balance out, usually with the changing of the seasons, when I'm stressed, or after the holidays if I've been eating extravagantly.

Juicing is ideal for people with digestive disorders and who have difficulty eating fiber-rich foods. It's also an easy way to get your daily recommended fruits and vegetables all in one glass.

If you want to try an all-day juice fast, alternate between fruit and vegetable juices so you don't get too much sugar but have enough calories to get through the day. I get unbelievable energy and mental clarity when I juice. If you feel weak, then you might not be drinking enough or you might be experiencing detox symptoms.

Some of the best produce to juice is listed below.

FRUITS
Apples
Pears
Oranges
Grapefruits
Lemons
Limes
Pineapples
Watermelons with rind
Cantaloupe with rind
Honeydew with rind
Grapes

VEGETABLES
Cucumbers
Celery
Zucchini
Beets and green tops
Carrots and green tops
Kale
Spinach
Swiss chard
Arugula
Lettuce

Parsley
Sprouts (sunflower, broccoli, alfalfa, etc.)
Bell peppers
Cabbage
Tomatoes
Radishes

OTHERS
Wheatgrass
Burdock root
Aloe vera
Garlic
Ginger
Dill
Mint
Cayenne pepper
Cinnamon (ground)

Hard to juice: peaches, plums, apricots, cherries, berries
Don't juice: bananas, avocados

Juice Recipes

OUR DAILY GREENS

1 large cucumber

8 stalks celery

Handful of kale

Handful of spinach

Handful of parsley

¼ lemon with rind

1 1-inch (2.5 cm) piece fresh ginger

CELLULITE SMOOTHER

2 large grapefruits

1 small orange

SUMMER COOLER

5 cups (750 g) chopped
watermelon with rind

1 fennel bulb and stalk

APPLE CIDER

2 apples

8 stalks celery

Dash of cinnamon

LIVER CLEANSE

1 beet

1 apple

1 cucumber

1 2-inch (5 cm) piece fresh ginger

½ lemon with rind

Handful of parsley

SKIN SAVER

2 cucumbers

1 10-inch (25 cm) piece
burdock root

1 apple

BRIGHT EYES

4 large carrots

2 oranges

NUTRITION NOTE: Juice Feasting has become quite popular in the raw food world. It usually involves a three-month juice fast for intense cleansing and weight loss. Any juicing over fourteen days should be done cautiously and preferably under the guidance of someone who is trained in long-term juice fasting. Fasting can slow your metabolism, so it's important to reintroduce foods gradually back into your diet so as not to shock your digestive system or create rapid weight gain.

In February 2007, I completed a 92-day juice feast, having lived on at least a gallon (4 L) a day of fresh raw juice for the past three months. This three-month "Feast" was easily one of the most transformative periods of my life, though when I first heard of the idea of Juice Feasting from David Rain, the creator of the JuiceFeasting.com program, I thought he was maybe a few carrots short of a juice!

I experienced such clarity, connectedness, creativity, and cleansing while Juice Feasting; meditation while on the Feast was super-intense, with so little "obstruction" in my system. Guidance was flowing through very clearly. Juice Feasting helped me move along rapidly on my own journey of cleansing and self-inquiry.

I thoroughly recommend Juice Feasting to people looking to give their digestive system a break for a while, to focus instead on detox and connecting more to their true inner core. I feel that Juice Feasting is an amazing gift to the self and it does not "need" to be done for ninety-two days— start with just 1–3 days and see how you feel . . . ENJOY!

A few recommended juice combos:

* "chocolate milk"—spinach/romaine/carrot
* celery/apple/cucumber/ginger—very light and refreshing
* pineapple with greens
* straight watermelon juice (with rind if organic)

—*Angela Stokes-Monarch, author and speaker, www.rawreform.com*

Breakfast

Living, whole foods are going to power you through the day much better than a gluten- and dairy-filled breakfast will. In my world, breakfast never tasted so good. Here are a few classic, and not so classic, morning favorites.

Maple-Pecan Granola

Makes about 12 cups
Soak time: 4 hours
Prep time: 20 minutes
Drying time: about 24 hours

This high-protein granola is great as a cereal or a travel snack. If you don't have palm sugar, use an additional ½ cup (170 g) of maple syrup or agave nectar. Your dehydrating time will be a bit longer, though.

2 cups (200 g) pecans, soaked 4 hours, coarsely chopped

2 cups (328 g) hulled buckwheat groats, soaked 1 hour, rinsed well

1 cup (168 g) flaxseeds, soaked 1 hour in 1¼ cups (295 ml) water; do not drain soak water

2 cups (160 g) rolled oats

1 cup (168 g) hemp seeds

1½ cups (180 g) dried cranberries or raisins

½ cup (170 g) maple syrup or agave nectar

½ cup (60 g) palm sugar

2 tablespoons (30 ml) vanilla extract

1 tablespoon (7 g) ground cinnamon

1 teaspoon sea salt

Combine all the ingredients in a large bowl and divide among 4 dehydrator trays lined with nonstick sheets (3 cups [300 g] per tray). Dehydrate at 110°F (43°C) for 12 hours. Flip the granola onto mesh screens and continue drying for another 12 hours or until crispy.

Store in an airtight container for 1 month. If it gets stale, dehydrate again until crisp.

NUTRITION NOTE: Buckwheat is gluten free and suitable for people with wheat allergies. Technically, it's a seed, not a grain, and is a great source of complete protein, omega-3 fatty acids, B vitamins, and minerals.

Berries and Cream Crepes

Makes 6 servings
Soak time: 2 hours
Prep time: 30 minutes
Drying time: 6 hours

This is a fun treat I like to serve for brunch and special occasions.

CREPES

4 bananas

1 tablespoon (15 ml) lemon juice

1/8 teaspoon cinnamon

CREAM

2 cups (240 g) cashews, soaked 2 hours

1/2 cup (120 ml) water

1/4 cup (85 g) agave nectar

1/2 vanilla bean, scraped

RASPBERRY SAUCE

2 cups (250 g) fresh or frozen raspberries, thawed

2 tablespoons (40 g) agave nectar

ADDITIONAL FILLING

2 cups (340 g) quartered strawberries

2 cups (290 g) blueberries

CREPES

1. Place all ingredients in a food processor and blend until smooth.
2. Pour batter 1/3 cup (80 ml) at a time onto a nonstick dehydrator sheet (a).
3. Use a small offset spatula to form into 6-inch (15-cm) disks (b). Makes about 6 to 8 crepes.
4. Dry at 110°F (43°C) for 6 hours or until dry but still pliable.
5. No need to transfer to a mesh screen as long as you can peel the crepes from the nonstick sheet without sticking (c).

CREAM

1. Process the cashews, water, agave nectar, and vanilla in a high-power blender until smooth. Add more water if too thick, 1 tablespoon (15 ml) at a time.
2. Chill at least 2 hours to firm.

SAUCE

Place all ingredients in a food processor and blend until smooth.

ADDITIONAL FILLING

To assemble, spread cream in the center of each crepe. Add fruit and fold sides toward center, like a cannoli. Drizzle the raspberry sauce over the crepes, top with additional fruit, and serve.

Stored separately, crepes and cream will keep for one week in the refrigerator.

a
b
c

Orange-Cranberry Oatmeal Scones

Makes 8 servings
Soak time: 8 to 12 hours
Prep time: 10 minutes
Drying time: 5 to 6 hours

Orange cranberry is one of my absolute favorite flavor combinations, and it's unbelievably delicious in this moist and chewy oatmeal-based recipe. I enjoy these for breakfast as well as for dessert paired with a warm cup of herbal tea.

1½ cups (276 g) oat groats, soaked 8–12 hours or overnight, drained (will yield 2 cups [370 g])

¾ cup (109 g) soft Medjool dates

1 teaspoon grated orange zest or 1 teaspoon orange extract

½ cup (60 g) dried cranberries

½ cup (50 g) walnuts, soaked 6–8 hours and dehydrated, chopped

1. Place the well-drained oats into a food processor and process until the oats break down and begin to stick (a). Scrape down the sides with a spatula if needed.
2. Add the dates and orange zest (b) and process until the mixture balls up into a dough (c).
3. Transfer to a mixing bowl and combine the cranberries and walnuts by hand.
4. Place the mixture in the center of a nonstick surface and press the dough into a ¾-inch (2 cm) to 1-inch-high (2.5 cm) round shape (d & e). A rolling pin is helpful for this as well.
5. Cut the round into 8 wedges (f) and transfer to a mesh dehydrator tray.
6. Dehydrate at 110°F (43°C) for 5 to 6 hours. If you like a moister scone, take them out after 5 hours. Scones will keep for 5 to 7 days in an airtight container in the refrigerator or for 1 month in the freezer.

NUTRITION NOTE: Oats have long been known as an excellent source of soluble fiber, which is great for digestion, balancing blood sugar, and lowering cholesterol. Oats are also high in protein; in immune-boosting minerals such as selenium and zinc; and in bone-building calcium, phosphorus, and magnesium. Commercial oats do contain a small amount of gluten. If you are gluten sensitive, you can order certified gluten-free oat groats from glutenfreeoats.com.

a   b   c   d   e   f

Seasonal Fruit Salad

Makes 2 servings
Prep time: 15 minutes

Use any seasonal fruits to make this simple yet elegant breakfast.

1 cup (150 g) quartered figs

1 cup (145 g) halved strawberries

1 cup (110 g) cored and sliced apples

⅓ cup (33 g) walnut halves, soaked 6–8 hours and dehydrated

⅓ cup (40 g) dried cherries or raisins

¼ cup (24 g) fresh mint, torn

2 tablespoons (40 g) raw honey

1. In a medium-size bowl, toss together the figs, strawberries, apples, walnuts, cherries, and mint and divide between 2 serving bowls.
2. Drizzle each with 1 tablespoon (20 g) of honey and serve.

Chia Pudding

Makes 2 or 3 servings
Prep time: 5 minutes
Soak time: 4 to 6 hours

This tapioca-like pudding is one of my breakfast favorites because it keeps me feeling full for hours. Try adding fresh fruit or dried fruit and nuts for variation. You can also substitute nut milk with fresh young Thai coconut water.

⅓ cup (50 g) chia seeds

2 cups (475 ml) Basic Nut Milk (see page 160)

2 tablespoons (40 g) agave nectar or honey, or pinch of stevia

Dash of cinnamon for garnish (optional)

Place the chia seeds and agave nectar in a bowl and cover them with the nut milk. Stir and let sit for 5 to 10 minutes. Stir again and then place in the refrigerator for 4 to 6 hours or overnight. Add more chia seeds if you like it thicker or add more nut milk to thin. Garnish with cinnamon.

The pudding will keep for 2 to 3 days in the refrigerator.

NUTRITION NOTE: Chia seeds were the food of the ancient Aztecs. They are high in protein, fiber, essential fatty acids, and calcium. Soaked chia is extremely hydrating and great for blood sugar balance. Avoid eating unsoaked chia seeds, because they can actually dehydrate you.

Salads and Dressings

With all the different types of greens, herbs and vegetables out there, you never have to have the same salad twice. Here are a dozen flavorful salads that go way beyond your typical garden salad.

Simply Splendid Kale Salad

Makes 4 servings
Prep time: 20 minutes

Kale is one of those greens that can be pretty tough to eat raw but is absolutely delicious when massaged with a little bit of sea salt and lemon juice. The cranberries help cut some of the bitterness while the flax oil gives it a nutty flavor and an extra kick of essential fatty acids. Substitute additional olive oil if you don't have flax oil on hand.

2 small bunches flat or curly kale, stems removed

2 tablespoons (30 ml) lemon juice

½ teaspoon sea salt

1 cup (180 g) tomatoes sliced into wedges

½ cup (70 g) pine nuts

½ cup (60 g) dried cranberries or raisins

1 tablespoon (15 ml) olive oil

1 tablespoon (15 ml) flax oil

Freshly ground black pepper (optional)

1. Chiffonade the kale and place it into a mixing bowl with the lemon juice and sea salt. Massage well with your hands, working the lemon juice and salt into the greens until softened.

2. Add the tomatoes, pine nuts, cranberries, olive oil, and flax oil and toss gently. Season to taste with pepper.

The salad will keep for 3 days in the refrigerator.

NUTRITION NOTE: Besides being a good source of vitamins A, C, and E and minerals, kale is also a very good source of usable calcium. Kale has been shown to provide substantial anticancer properties and has phytonutrients that activate enzymes in the liver to help the body detoxify and cleanse. For many, myself included, kale is a raw foodist's best friend.

Dandelion Salad

My favorite brunch spot in New York City is the Roebling Tea Room in Williamsburg, Brooklyn. I loved their house salad so much I created my own version so I could enjoy it at home. The dates balance out the bitterness of the dandelion greens while the simple dressing gives it some zip.

DRESSING

3 tablespoons (45 ml) olive oil

3 tablespoons (45 g) red wine vinegar

¹⁄₈ teaspoon sea salt

SALAD

2 medium-size grapefruits, supremed

¹⁄₃ celery root bulb

6 cups (110 g) (2 small bunches) dandelion greens, washed, ends trimmed

1 cup (145 g) Medjool dates, pitted and quartered lengthwise

DRESSING

For the dressing, whisk the olive oil, red wine vinegar, and sea salt in small bowl.

TO SUPREME A GRAPEFRUIT:

1. Slice off the top and bottom with a knife (a).
2. Place the bottom flat side of the fruit on the cutting board and carefully cut the peel from top to bottom, following the curvature of the fruit, removing the white pith (b).
3. Cut down along each section to the center of the grapefruit (c).
4. Turn the knife to loosen each section and lift it out (d). Remove all remaining sections the same way.

TO PREPARE THE CELERY ROOT:

1. Wash the celery root, and then peel the rough outer skin with a sharp knife.
2. Thinly slice the celery root bulb with a mandoline or knife.

SALAD

Cut the longer dandelion greens in half and then gently combine them with the dates, grapefruit sections, celery root slices, and dressing in a large bowl.

The salad is best eaten the day it is made. The dressing, stored separately, will keep for at least 2 weeks in an airtight container in the refrigerator.

NUTRITION NOTE: Health experts cite dandelion greens as one of the superstars of the vegetable world. It has long been used in herbal traditions as a liver detoxifier, it is a natural diuretic, and it has been proven useful in helping heartburn and indigestion and as an aid in reducing high blood pressure.

Chef's Tip: "Supreme" is the culinary term for removing the rind, pith, membrane, and seeds of citrus fruits.

a   b   c   d

Jicama-Papaya-Mango Salad

Makes 4 servings
Prep time: 30 minutes

Lime and cayenne take this fruit salad to another level. This is also the perfect salad for a detox diet; just omit the olive oil and salt. For best results use chilled (not frozen) fruit.

4 cups (560 g) cubed papaya

2 cups (260 g) julienned jicama

1 mango, diced

1 small shallot, sliced paper thin

1 tablespoon (6 g) chopped mint

1 tablespoon (1 g) chopped cilantro

⅓ cup (80 ml) lime juice

2 tablespoons (30 ml) olive oil

¼ teaspoon sea salt

⅛ teaspoon cayenne pepper

4 cups (120 g) baby spinach

PREPARING JICAMA:

1. To prepare the jicama, slice the bottom and the top flat with a chef's knife (a).
2. Remove the brown skin by cutting carefully around the curvature (b).
3. Slice in half crosswise.
4. Use the julienne feature on your mandoline or slice thinly by hand (c).

DICING MANGO:

1. Slice the wide sides of the mango vertically, being careful not to cut into the pit (d), about 1 inch (2.5 cm) or more, depending on the size of the fruit.
2. Score into cubes carefully without slicing into the skin (e).
3. Invert the mango piece (f) and cut away pieces with a knife (g).

SALAD

1. Place the papaya, jicama, mango, shallot, mint, and cilantro into a large bowl and set aside.
2. Whisk together the lime juice, olive oil, salt, and cayenne and pour over the fruit. Toss very gently and serve over a bed of baby spinach.

The salad will keep for 1 day in the refrigerator.

Chef's Tip: Jicama is a root vegetable similar to a potato that has a sweet, nutty flavor. It adds a great crunch to salads and is a very good source of vitamin C and fiber.

e   f   g

Spinach Pear Salad with Maple-Cinnamon Vinaigrette

Makes 4 to 6 servings
Prep time: 15 minutes

This is a quick and simple salad that tastes wonderfully gourmet.

SALAD

6 cups (330 g) packed baby spinach

1 cup (220 g) coarsely chopped pecans

½ cup (60 g) dried cranberries or raisins

1 small shallot, thinly sliced

2 pears, thinly sliced

DRESSING

½ cup (120 ml) olive oil

3 tablespoons (45 ml) balsamic vinegar

3 tablespoons (60 g) maple syrup

¼ teaspoon cinnamon

¼ teaspoon sea salt

1. Place all the salad ingredients except the pears in a large bowl and set aside.
2. Whisk all the dressing ingredients in a bowl. Pour over the salad and toss gently.
3. Place the salad on individual plates and top with the sliced pears.

Salad will keep for 1 day.

NUTRITION NOTE: Popeye's favorite food truly is a superfood. Spinach is loaded with minerals, vitamins, and phytonutrients that offer countless health benefits, such as protecting the heart, gastrointestinal system, prostate, brain function, and eyes.

Mediterranean Hemp Seed Tabbouleh

Makes 4 servings
Prep time: 15 minutes

Hemp seeds make a great substitute for the traditionally used wheat bulgur and are an excellent source of complete protein and essential fatty acids. Zante currants are a type of mini raisin and give this dish an unexpected hint of sweetness. If you prefer a more traditional tabbouleh, you can omit them.

2 big bunches parsley

¼ cup (24 g) fresh mint

½ cup (84 g) hemp seeds

1 large tomato, seeded and diced

¼ cup (60 ml) lemon juice

¼ cup (38 g) dried Zante currants (optional)

2 tablespoons (30 ml) olive oil

2 tablespoons (20 g) chopped yellow onion

1 teaspoon sea salt

1. Place the parsley and mint in a food processor and pulse several times until well chopped.
2. Transfer to a mixing bowl and add the hemp seeds, tomato, lemon juice, currants, oil, onion, and salt. Toss well and serve.

The tabbouleh will keep for 1 day in the refrigerator.

NUTRITION NOTE: Parsley is one of the top medicinal herbs out there. A great digestive aid, parsley cleanses the liver and the kidney, purifies the blood, may protect against rheumatoid arthritis, and is chock-full of vitamins, minerals, and antioxidants.

Thai Green Bean Salad

Makes 4 servings
Prep time: 25 minutes

This crisp and bold-tasting salad is always a hit at potlucks. I like to prepare the dressing the traditional Thai way by using a mortar and pestle. If you don't own one, mincing the ingredients with a knife will do just fine.

4 cups (300 g) sugar snap peas

1 cup (180 g) diced tomatoes

⅓ cup (55 g) diced red onion

2 cloves garlic

½–inch (1 cm) piece ginger, peeled and chopped

1 small dried red Thai chile pepper

¼ cup (60 ml) lime juice

1 tablespoon (20 g) agave nectar

1 teaspoon sea salt

2 tablespoons (18 g) wild jungle peanuts

1. Slice the sugar snap peas on an angle to create a diamond shape (a). In a medium-size mixing bowl combine the sugar snap peas with the diced tomatoes and red onion.

2. In a mortar, grind the garlic, ginger, and red Thai chile thoroughly (b). If you are sensitive to hot spice, use half a pepper, omit it from the recipe, or substitute with a pinch of red pepper flakes.

3. In a small bowl combine the lime juice, agave nectar, and sea salt with the crushed garlic, ginger, and chile. Add the dressing to the sugar snap peas, tomatoes, and red onion and combine well.

4. In the mortar, coarsely grind the wild jungle peanuts and sprinkle on top of the salad.

This salad is best the day it is made.

NUTRITION NOTE: Wild jungle peanuts are raw, South American peanuts that are high in protein and free of the allergen aflatoxin. They're becoming increasingly popular at health food stores. See "Resources" on page 189 for where to find them online.

a   b

Beet and Watercress Salad with Sweet Miso Dressing

Makes 4 to 6 servings
Prep time: 25 minutes

Beets and watercress are both excellent blood cleansers and are prized for their multitude of medicinal uses. Raw beets also cleanse the liver and the intestines and can protect against stomach cancer. Watercress is widely used as a culinary as well as a medicinal herb. For centuries it has been known to be a blood builder, aphrodisiac, and diuretic, among countless other medicinal benefits. It also has anticancer properties and contains iodine, which is essential for supporting thyroid function.

DRESSING

1 tablespoon (16 g) chickpea miso or sweet or light miso paste

1 tablespoon (20 g) agave nectar

1 tablespoon (30 ml) balsamic vinegar

2 tablespoons (30 ml) Basic Nut Milk (see page 160)

¼ cup (60 ml) flax or olive oil

SALAD

6 cups (330 g) chopped, packed watercress

⅓ cup (55 g) thinly sliced red onion

2 avocados, sliced

1 small beet, spiralized or julienned

2 teaspoons black sesame seeds

DRESSING
Process all the ingredients in a blender until smooth.

SALAD

1. In a large bowl, toss the watercress and onion with the dressing and divide among 4 to 6 serving plates.

2. Top each plate with the sliced avocados and beets and sprinkle with the sesame seeds.

Chef's Tip: If you can't find watercress in your area, substitute with a spring salad mix.

Salad will keep 1 day.

Marinated Yellow Summer Squash

Makes 4 to 6 servings
Prep time: 20 minutes

Yellow squash has a more mild, delicate flavor than zucchini and is an excellent source of manganese and vitamin C. It's very low in calories and high in fiber and water content, making it the perfect diet food.

SALAD

3 yellow summer squash

⅓ cup (55 g) thinly sliced red onion

1 tablespoon (4 g) chopped fresh parsley

1 teaspoon fresh thyme

DRESSING

3 tablespoons (45 ml) lemon juice

3 tablespoons (45 ml) olive oil

¼ teaspoon sea salt

Pinch of black pepper

SALAD

Use a mandoline to slice the summer squash into very thin strips. Add to a bowl with the sliced onion, parsley, and thyme.

DRESSING

In a small bowl whisk together the lemon juice, olive oil, sea salt, and pepper and pour over the squash. Toss gently and let sit for 1 hour.

The squash will keep for 2 days in the refrigerator.

Raw Power Salad

Makes 4 to 6 servings
Prep time: 25 minutes

Protein rich and extremely satisfying, this superhero salad is one of my favorites. I like to vary my greens every day, so use whatever greens you have on hand, such as romaine, spring mix, Swiss chard, or even cabbage.

SALAD

2 cups (60 g) packed baby spinach

2 cups (110 g) packed red leaf lettuce

2 cups (110 g) packed, shredded kale

2 small avocados, sliced

1 cup (50 g) broccoli sprouts

1 cup (50 g) sunflower sprouts or additional 1 cup (50 g) broccoli or other sprout

2 cups (360 g) chopped tomatoes

⅔ cup (74 g) dulse strips

½ cup (84 g) hemp seeds

1 teaspoon spirulina or blue-green algae

¼ cup Protein Crunch Mix (optional; see page 154)

DRESSING

3 tablespoons (45 ml) lemon juice

3 tablespoons (45 ml) flax oil

1 teaspoon crushed garlic

Sea salt to taste

SALAD
Combine all the ingredients in a large bowl.

DRESSING
Whisk all the dressing ingredients together and pour over the salad. Toss gently.

The salad will keep for 1 day in the refrigerator.

NUTRITION NOTE: Spirulina and blue-green algae are a bit of an acquired taste. Try just a sprinkle and work your way up, and soon you might find yourself craving it. Both are high in complete protein and B vitamins, including B_{12}.

Seedy Avocado-Tomato-Corn Salad

Makes 4 to 6 servings
Prep time: 30 minutes

This salad reminds me of early summer in Southern California when corn comes into season. Raw corn is crunchy and sweet and absolutely delicious in this zesty salad.

SALAD

1 ear corn

2 cups (300 g) halved grape tomatoes

½ cup (80 g) diced red onion

¼ cup (4 g) chopped cilantro

2 tablespoons (18 g) sunflower seeds

2 tablespoons (18 g) pumpkin seeds

2 avocados, cut into 1-inch (2.5 cm) cubes

DRESSING

¼ cup (60 ml) lime juice

2 tablespoons (30 ml) olive oil

½ teaspoon sea salt

Dash of cayenne pepper

SALAD

1. Use a knife to remove the corn kernels. Place in a bowl with the tomatoes, onion, cilantro, and seeds and toss well.

2. Gently fold in the avocados.

DRESSING

Whisk all the ingredients together and pour over the salad. Toss gently.

This salad will keep for 2 days in the refrigerator.

Vietnamese Salad

Makes 4 to 6 servings
Prep time: 45 minutes

I love Vietnamese cuisine for its wide use of fresh herbs. This recipe utilizes generous amounts of fresh watercress, basil, mint, and cilantro among Asian greens and a light and tangy dressing.

SALAD

3 cups (165 g) packed, chopped bok choy leaves

3 cups (270 g) packed, shredded napa cabbage leaves

1 cup (55 g) packed, coarsely chopped watercress

1 cup (130 g) julienned carrots

1 cup (135 g) chopped cucumbers

½ cup (88 g) thinly sliced radishes

½ cup (20 g) basil, torn

½ cup (48 g) mint, torn

½ cup (8 g) cilantro, torn

1 shallot, thinly sliced

DRESSING

¼ cup (60 ml) lime juice

3 tablespoons (45 ml) brown rice vinegar

2 tablespoons (30 ml) sesame oil

1 tablespoon (80 g) palm sugar

1 tablespoon (8 g) grated ginger

2 teaspoons crushed garlic

½ teaspoon sea salt

SALAD

Combine all the ingredients in a large bowl.

DRESSING

1. Whisk all the dressing ingredients in a bowl, pour over the salad, and toss gently.

2. Allow to sit for 15 minutes for the flavors to mingle. Toss again and serve.

The salad will keep for 1 day in the refrigerator.

Wild Arugula Orange-Fennel Salad

Makes 4 to 6 servings
Prep time: 30 minutes

Wild arugula has a spicy, mustardlike flavor that is balanced out by the orange slices and pomegranate seeds in this recipe. If you prefer a milder salad, choose baby arugula, which is much more tender and mellower tasting.

SALAD

6 cups (120 g) packed wild or baby arugula

3 oranges, supremed, (see page 72 for how to supreme)

1 bulb fennel, thinly sliced

¾ cup (109 g) pomegranate seeds

¾ cup (75 g) chopped walnuts

1 shallot, sliced

DRESSING

½ cup (120 ml) orange juice

¼ cup (60 ml) olive oil

Sea salt to taste

SALAD
Combine all the ingredients in a large bowl.

DRESSING
Whisk all the ingredients together and pour over the salad. Toss gently.

The salad will keep for 2 days in the refrigerator.

NUTRITION NOTE: Arugula, like other dark greens, is high in chlorophyll, vitamins, and minerals and contains anticancer phytonutrients, glucosinolates, and sulforaphanes, which are responsible for helping the body remove toxins and carcinogens.

Salad Dressings

HONEY–WHOLE GRAIN MUSTARD DRESSING

Makes 1½ cups (355 ml)   Prep time: 10 minutes

1 cup (60 ml) olive oil
¼ cup (60 g) raw liquid honey or agave nectar
2½ tablespoons (17 g) whole grain mustard
1½ tablespoons (22 ml) apple cider vinegar
¼ teaspoon sea salt
fresh ground pepper to taste

Whisk olive oil, honey, mustard, vinegar, and sea salt until combined, or use a mini blender if the honey is too thick to whisk. The dressing will keep for two weeks in the refrigerator.

SUNFLOWER SEED DRESSING

Makes about 2 cups (470 ml)   Soak time: 4 hours
Prep time: 10 minutes

1 cup (145 g) sunflower seeds, soaked 4 hours
⅔ cup (160 ml) water
¼ cup (60 ml) lemon juice
2 tablespoons (30 ml) tamari
1 tablespoon (20 g) agave nectar
2 small cloves garlic
½ teaspoon dried Italian herbs

Place all the ingredients in a blender and process until smooth. The dressing will keep for 1 week in the refrigerator.

BASIL VINAIGRETTE

Makes 1⅓ cups (315 ml)   Prep time: 5 minutes

1 cup (235 ml) olive oil
⅓ cup (13 g) fresh basil
¼ cup (60 ml) apple cider vinegar
2 tablespoons (40 g) agave nectar
1 clove garlic
¼ teaspoon sea salt

Place all the ingredients in a blender and process until smooth. The dressing will keep for 1 week in the refrigerator.

FAT-FREE TOMATO DRESSING

Makes 1½ cups (355 ml)   Prep time: 10 minutes

2 large tomatoes, chopped
1 tablespoon (15 ml) lemon juice
1 tablespoon (10 g) chopped shallot
1 Medjool date
¾ teaspoon sea salt

Place all the ingredients in a blender and process until smooth. The dressing will keep for 2 days in the refrigerator.

CREAMY DILL DRESSING

Makes 2 cups (475 ml)   Soak time: 2 hours
Prep time: 10 minutes

2 cups (240 g) cashews, soaked 2 hours
1 cup (235 ml) water
2 tablespoons (40 g) agave nectar
1 tablespoon (16 g) tamarind paste
2 cloves garlic (optional)
2 teaspoons sea salt
3 tablespoons (12 g) fresh chopped dill or 1 table-spoon (3 g) dried dill

In a blender, process the cashews, water, agave nectar, tamarind paste, garlic, and sea salt until smooth. Pulse with the dill until combined. The dressing will keep for 1 week in the refrigerator.

GARLIC TAHINI DRESSING

Makes 1½ cups (355 ml)   Prep time: 10 minutes

1 cup (240 g) raw tahini paste
⅔ cup (160 ml) water
⅓ cup (80 ml) lemon juice
3 cloves garlic, pressed
1 teaspoon sea salt
¼ teaspoon black pepper

Place all the ingredients in a blender and process until smooth. The dressing will keep in the refrigerator for 1 week and will thicken during storage. Add 1 tablespoon (15 ml) of water at a time to thin. Great for salads, wraps, or BBQ Veggie Burgers (see page 122).

Soups and Sides

The beauty of raw soup is that most only take a few minutes to prepare and can keep you feeling full for hours. If you prefer a warm soup you can blend it longer or warm it gently on the stove top. This section contains some of my best soup recipes as well as some side dishes to pair with them or with an entrée.

Thai Coconut Soup

Makes 4 servings
Prep time: 45 minutes
Warming time: 1 to 2 hours

Lemon, lime, and coconut create a symphony of flavor in this delicious, creamy soup. Thai peppers are quite hot, so feel free to leave them out or substitute with a generous pinch of crushed red pepper flakes. Some ingredients might look unfamiliar, but they can easily be found at most Asian food markets.

4 cups (340 g) unsweetened desiccated coconut

4½ cups (1,058 ml) hot water

¼ cup (60 ml) lime juice

¼ cup (60 ml) lemon juice

¼ cup (4 g) chopped lemongrass

2 tablespoons (40 g) agave nectar

¼ fresh Thai chile pepper, seeded (optional)

1½ teaspoons sea salt

1 teaspoon grated galangal or ginger

4 kaffir lime leaves

1½ cups (130 g) thinly sliced baby bok choy

1 cup (130 g) julienned carrots

1 cup (180 g) diced tomatoes

2 tablespoons (2 g) chopped cilantro

1. In a food processor, process the coconut until finely ground (a).
2. Add the hot water to the food processor and blend for 30 to 60 seconds (b).
3. Strain the coconut milk through a nut milk bag (c & d). Depending on the size of your food processor, you may have to do this step in small batches. *Note the liquid level line on your food processor container and do not exceed it.*
4. In a blender, add the strained coconut milk, lime juice, lemon juice, lemongrass, agave nectar, chile pepper, sea salt, galangal, and kaffir lime leaves and blend well. Taste the soup and adjust the ingredients if it needs more sweet, sour, spice, or salt.
5. Pour the soup through a fine mesh strainer into a medium-size bowl.

recipe continues...

a　b　c　d

6. Add the bok choy, carrots, tomatoes, and cilantro to the soup (e) and place the entire bowl in the dehydrator for 1 hour at 145°F (63°C), then lower to 110°F (43°C) for another hour or until warm enough to your liking.

The soup will keep for 3 days in the refrigerator.

NOTE: Be very careful when handling chile peppers. Use a designated cutting board for hot peppers and wash your hands very well afterward, or better yet, wear disposable gloves.

TO PREPARE LEMONGRASS:

1. Remove the bottom base root and most of the top green portion with a knife (a).
2. Remove the outer layer (b).
3. Thinly slice until you no longer see the purple rings (c).

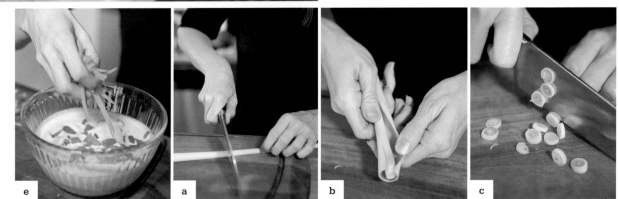

e   a   b   c

Spiced Carrot–Butternut Squash Soup with Pine Nut Cream

Makes 4 servings
Soak time: 2 hours
Prep time: 40 minutes

Pine nut cream perfectly ties the sweetness of the carrots with the leeks and spices in this hearty autumn soup.

PINE NUT CREAM

1 cup (135 g) pine nuts, soaked 2 hours

¼ cup (60 ml) water

2 tablespoons (30 ml) lemon juice

¼ teaspoon sea salt

Dash of white pepper

SOUP

3 cups (710 ml) fresh carrot juice

¾ cup (105 g) cubed butternut squash

¼ cup (25 g) sliced leeks

1½ teaspoons pumpkin pie spice

1 teaspoon fresh thyme

¾ teaspoon sea salt

Pinch of black pepper

¾ medium-size avocado

CREAM
Place all the ingredients into a high-power blender and process until completely smooth.

SOUP
1. Place the carrot juice, squash, leeks, pumpkin pie spice, thyme, salt, and pepper into a high-power blender and process until smooth. If you like a warm soup, blend for 2 minutes. Add the avocado and blend again until smooth.
2. Pour into soup bowls and serve with the pine nut cream.

The soup will keep for 3 or 4 days in the refrigerator. Pine nut cream will keep about a week in the refrigerator.

Chef's Tip: You can use store-bought organic carrot juice and precut butternut squash if you're in a pinch for time.

NUTRITION NOTE: Carrot juice is high in beta-carotene, a phytonutrient the body converts into vitamin A, a powerful antioxidant responsible for reducing free-radical damage and maintaining eye health, liver function, and bone formation.

Cucumber Gazpacho

Makes 4 or 5 servings
Prep time: 20 minutes
Chill time: 1 hour

Gazpacho is a chilled vegetable soup that is usually enjoyed in the summer months. It is light, lemony, refreshing, and tasty, and it's perfect if you're on a simple raw food cleanse.

4 cups (270 g) chopped cucumber (2 medium)

2 cups (475 ml) water

1 cup (100 g) chopped celery

¼ cup (60 ml) lemon juice

2 tablespoons (8 g) fresh dill, plus a few sprigs for garnish

1¼ teaspoons sea salt

½ large avocado

4 Roma tomatoes, diced

1 cup (160 g) diced sweet or white onion

Freshly ground pepper to taste

1. Process the cucumbers, water, celery, lemon juice, dill, and sea salt in a blender until smooth. Add the avocado and blend again. Don't blend too long or your soup may turn to mousse.

2. Pour the soup into a large bowl or container, add the tomatoes and onion, and chill for at least 1 hour.

3. To serve, pour the soup into individual serving bowls. Add freshly ground pepper to taste and garnish with the dill sprigs.

The gazpacho will keep for 2 days in the refrigerator.

NUTRITION NOTE: I actually like to call this my beauty soup because it is so rich in silica, a mineral that strengthens connective tissues and gives your skin elasticity. Avocados contain vitamins C and E, which protect, hydrate, and nourish your skin. Tomatoes help improve skin texture and color, and the sulfur in onions promotes collagen formation, mineralized hair, and a beautiful complexion. If you eat this soup regularly, don't be surprised if friends comment on your glowing skin!

Creamy Tomato-Basil Soup

Makes 4 to 6 servings
Prep time: 20 minutes

Classic comfort food made easy.

6 cups (1 kg) seeded and chopped tomatoes

1½ cups (355 ml) Basic Nut Milk (see page 160)

¼ cup (10 g) fresh basil or 4 teaspoons dried

2 tablespoons (8 g) fresh oregano or 2 teaspoons dried

1 tablespoon (20 g) agave nectar or 2 Medjool dates

1½ teaspoons sea salt

½ teaspoon crushed garlic

2 tablespoons (30 ml) olive oil

Freshly ground pepper to taste

1. Place the tomatoes, nut milk, basil, oregano, agave, salt, and garlic into a blender and process until smooth.
2. While the blender is running, pour the olive oil in slowly to emulsify. For warm soup, blend for 2 minutes.
3. Pour into serving bowls and garnish with the pepper.

The soup will keep for 2 days in the refrigerator.

Miso Soup

Makes 4 servings
Prep time: 15 minutes

Miso is a traditional Japanese seasoning made by fermenting soy, rice, barley, or beans. I prefer to use chickpea miso, but you can experiment with other types, which all have different flavors. Miso contains beneficial bacteria that can be damaged by cooking, so make sure your water isn't too hot. Miso also contains many trace minerals and a small amount of protein. If you're on a low-sodium diet, use a little less miso.

⅓ cup (83 g) chickpea miso or sweet or light miso paste

4 cups (940 ml) warm water

¼ cup (28 g) dried instant wakame flakes

¾ cup (53 g) sliced shiitake mushrooms

2 tablespoons (20 g) sliced scallions

1. In a large bowl combine the miso paste with a small amount of water and mix with a fork until it becomes liquid. Add the 4 cups warm water and mix well.

2. Add the wakame, mushrooms, and scallions and let sit for 5 minutes or more for the wakame to hydrate. Check the package label for the soak time.

3. Stir and then serve immediately.

The soup will keep for 2 days in the refrigerator.

Chef's Tip: For a heartier soup add ¼ cup (33 g) sliced carrots and ½ cup (88 g) spiralized daikon radish.

NUTRITION NOTE: Wakame is a mild-tasting seaweed with a flavor similar to that of spinach. Like other sea vegetables, wakame is rich in minerals and can help remove heavy metals, detoxify the body, and decrease the risk of cancer, according to health expert David Wolfe in his Longevity Now program.

Green Energy Soup

I like to enjoy this soup in place of a heavy dinner. It keeps me going till bedtime, and I sleep like a baby because my body isn't busy digesting food all night.

2 cups (475 ml) water

5 leaves kale, stems removed and chopped

2 tomatoes, chopped

½ cucumber, chopped

2 tablespoons (30 ml) lime juice

2 or 3 cloves garlic

1 teaspoon sea salt

Pinch of cayenne pepper (optional)

½ to 1 avocado

1 red bell pepper, diced

Freshly ground pepper to taste

1. Place the water, kale, tomatoes, cucumber, lime juice, garlic, sea salt, and cayenne into a blender and process until smooth. Add the ½ avocado and blend again. For a thicker soup, add a whole avocado.

2. Garnish the soup with the diced red bell pepper and ground pepper and serve.

The soup will keep for 1 day in the refrigerator.

Spinach-Walnut Pesto and Pignolia Cheese–Stuffed Mushrooms

Makes 6 to 8 servings
Soak time: 2 hours
Prep time: 40 minutes
Warming time: 2 to 4 hours

These are always the hit of the party. You can use baby portobellos or cremini mushrooms if you want to serve them as hors d'oeuvres. Just cut the dehydrating time down by 1 hour.

16 to 20 medium-size (preferable) or 5 to 6 large portobello mushrooms

MARINADE

2 tablespoons (30 ml) olive oil

2 tablespoons (30 ml) lemon juice

2 tablespoons (30 ml) tamari

¼ teaspoon sea salt

PIGNOLIA CHEESE

1 cup (135 g) pine nuts, soaked 2 hours

¼ cup (60 ml) water

1 tablespoon (15 ml) lemon juice

¼ teaspoon sea salt

SPINACH-WALNUT PESTO

2 cups (60 g) packed spinach

¼ cup (60 ml) olive oil

2 cloves garlic

1 tablespoon (15 ml) lemon juice

¼ teaspoon sea salt

½ cup (50 g) walnuts, soaked 6–8 hours and dehydrated

MUSHROOMS

Remove the mushroom stems by gently twisting them off. Mushrooms are like little sponges, so you don't want to rinse them in the sink; instead, use a lightly damp cloth to wipe off any dirt on the caps.

MARINADE

1. In a small bowl, combine all the marinade ingredients.
2. Place the mushrooms in a baking pan and pour the mixture over them. Use your hands to gently coat the mushrooms with marinade and set aside for 15 minutes. If using large mushrooms, let sit in the marinade for 1 hour.

CHEESE

Process all the ingredients in a blender until smooth. Add more water if needed, 1 tablespoon (15 ml) at a time, but it's best to keep it thick.

PESTO

Place the spinach, oil, garlic, lemon juice, and salt into a food processor and blend until smooth. Scrape down the sides of the container with a spatula as needed. Add the walnuts and pulse until incorporated but still chunky.

ASSEMBLY

For each mushroom cap, fill with pignolia cheese followed by a dollop of pesto. Place the stuffed mushrooms on a dehydrator tray lined with a non-stick sheet and warm at 110°F (43°C) for 2 to 3 hours. Add an hour if using large mushrooms. Serve immediately.

Leftover mushrooms will last for 3 days in the refrigerator and will reheat well in the dehydrator.

NUTRITION NOTE: Portobello mushrooms contain more potassium than bananas! Potassium is an important mineral and electrolyte that maintains regular heart rhythm, lowers blood pressure, brings oxygen to the brain, and decreases the risk of stroke and heart disease. Their meaty flavor and texture make them popular among vegetarians.

Ground Veggie Meat

Makes 2 cups
Prep time: 30 minutes
Drying time: 4 to 5 hours

Use this for Spaghetti Bolognese (see page 112) or in the Vegetarian Homestyle Chili (see page 127) or just enjoy it as a side.

1 cup (120 g) walnuts, soaked 6–8 hours and dehydrated

2 cups (240 g) shredded zucchini

1 cup (70 g) minced cremini or portobello mushrooms

¼ cup (40 g) minced white or yellow onion

¼ cup (15 g) minced parsley

2 tablespoons (30 ml) lemon juice

2 tablespoons (30 ml) tamari

Pinch of sea salt and freshly ground pepper

1. Place the walnuts in a food processor and process until coarsely ground.
2. Add the zucchini and pulse a few times, being careful not to overprocess (a). You don't want to turn it to mush.
3. Transfer to a mixing bowl, add the mushrooms, onion, parsley, lemon juice, tamari, salt, and pepper and mix well.
4. Spread over a dehydrator tray lined with a nonstick sheet and dry at 110°F (43°C) for 2 hours (b).
5. Transfer to a mesh screen and dehydrate for an additional 2 to 3 hours. Be careful not to overdry (c).
6. Return the ground veggie meat to a bowl and fluff with a fork. Serve warm.

The veggie meat will keep for 3 days in the refrigerator.

a   b   c

Zucchini Hummus

Makes 6 to 8 servings
Prep time: 15 minutes
Chill time: 2 hours

Traditional hummus is made with cooked chickpeas, which I've substituted with zucchini without sacrificing any of the fantastic flavor. Try it with Sun-Dried Tomato and Herb Flax Crackers (see page 151) or crudités.

1 cup (124 g) peeled and chopped zucchini

¼ cup (60 ml) lemon juice

2 tablespoons (30 ml) olive oil

3 cloves garlic

1 teaspoon sea salt

½ teaspoon paprika

½ teaspoon cumin

Pinch of cayenne pepper

½ cup (120 g) raw tahini paste

2 teaspoons minced parsley

Za'atar seasoning, paprika, olive oil, and pine nuts for garnish

1. Place the zucchini, lemon juice, oil, garlic, salt, paprika, cumin, and cayenne in a blender and process until smooth. Add the tahini and blend again until well incorporated.

2. Transfer to a bowl and stir in the minced parsley. Garnish with the za'atar seasoning, paprika, olive oil, and pine nuts.

3. Chill for 2 hours.

The hummus will keep for 3 days in the refrigerator.

NUTRITION NOTE: Tahini is made of ground sesame seeds and is used in many Middle Eastern dishes. Sesame seeds are a great source of B vitamins and calcium, which are even more bioavailable when ground into tahini paste. Two tablespoons (30 g) of tahini contains almost 35 percent of your recommended daily calcium intake.

Chef's Tip: Za'atar is a popular Middle Eastern seasoning made of dried thyme, oregano, marjoram, sesame seeds, and other spices. It's not essential for this dish, but it provides an authentic touch.

Mexican Wild Rice

This rice is great on its own, but it's even better with South-of-the-Border Soft Tacos (see page 103).

4 cups (660 g) bloomed wild rice (see page 44)

2 tablespoons (30 ml) lemon juice

2 tablespoons (30 ml) olive oil

1 teaspoon sea salt

1 teaspoon cumin

1/3 cup (37 g) sun-dried tomato powder*

1 cup (150 g) fresh corn kernels

1/3 cup (55 g) diced sweet yellow onion

1/3 cup (5 g) chopped cilantro

1. Place the wild rice in a medium-size bowl.
2. In a small bowl, combine the lemon juice, olive oil, sea salt, and cumin. Pour over the bloomed rice and combine well.
3. Add the sun-dried tomato powder and combine again.
4. Add the corn, onion, and cilantro, toss to combine, and serve. For warmed rice place in the dehydrator at 145°F (63°C) for 1 hour.

The rice will keep for 4 days in an airtight container in the refrigerator.

*To make sun-dried tomato powder, process dried tomatoes in a food processor or blender until it becomes a fine powder.

Basic Nut Cheese

Makes 8–12 servings
Soak time: varies
Prep time: 10 minutes
Fermentation time: 8–14 hours

Nut cheeses are a surprisingly tasty substitute for dairy cheese and can be used as a spread on crackers, breads, and wraps. This is the base that you can add your own personal touch to. Add your favorite fresh herbs, peppercorns, miso paste, olives, and seasonings, or sweeten it with agave nectar or fruit purée to create a dessert cheese. Nuts that work great as a base are:

* Cashews (soak 2 hours)
* Macadamia nuts (soak 2 hours)
* Pine nuts (soak 2 hours)
* Almonds* (soak 8 to 12 hours)

2 cups (290 g) nuts, soaked (see page 47 for soak times)

1 cup (235 ml) Rejuvelac (see page 167) or 1 cup (235 ml) warm water with ¼ teaspoon probiotic powder

BASE

In a blender, combine the nuts and rejuvelac until smooth.

1. Pour the cheese into a nut milk bag and set in a strainer for 8 to 14 hours to ferment at room temperature. Allow to ripen until it suits your taste.

2. Squeeze the excess water from the nut milk bag and transfer to a mixing bowl. Season or sweeten the cheese to your liking and store in a glass container in the refrigerator for up to 1 week.

*To remove almond skins, pour hot water over the almonds and allow to sit for 5 minutes. Cover with cool water and remove the skins by pinching the almonds. They should slide right off. Soak peeled almonds in cold water for the time listed above.

Herbed Cashew Hemp Cheese

Makes 8–12 servings
Soak time: 2 hours
Prep time: 10 minutes
Fermentation time: 8 to 14 hours
Chill time: 12 hours

Hemp seeds give this recipe a nice, nutty flavor while the herbs make this the freshest, tastiest cream cheese I've ever had.

1¾ cups (210 g) cashews, soaked 2 hours

¼ cup (42 g) hemp seeds

1 cup (235 ml) Rejuvelac (see page 167) or 1 cup (235 ml) warm water with ¼ teaspoon probiotic powder

1 tablespoon (3 g) minced chives

1 tablespoon (4 g) minced dill

¾ teaspoon sea salt

Dried Italian herbs to decorate (thyme, basil, oregano, rosemary)

1. Process the cashews and hemp seeds with the rejuvelac in a blender until smooth.
2. Pour the cheese into a nut milk bag (a) and set in a strainer for 8 to 14 hours to ferment at room temperature. Allow to ripen until it suits your taste.
3. Squeeze the excess water from the nut milk bag and transfer the cheese to a bowl. Add the chives, dill, and salt and mix well with a spoon.
4. Put the cheese into a 4½-inch (11-cm) springform pan (b) or a small bowl lined with plastic wrap and allow to firm up in the refrigerator for at least 12 hours (c).
5. Remove from the pan (d) and use an offset spatula (e) to shape up if necessary. Sprinkle with the dried herbs (f). Serve with crackers, bread, or crudités.

The cheese will keep for 3 or 4 days in the refrigerator.

a

b

c

d

e

f

Chunky Curried Guacamole

Makes 4 servings
Prep time: 10 minutes

I'm very fortunate to live near one of the best raw and vegan restaurants on the West Coast. Au Lac offers "humanese" cuisine prepared by the extraordinarily talented Chef Ito. His curried guacamole knocked my socks off and inspired me to make this bold and chunky version. It's so satisfying, I often eat half a batch wrapped in romaine leaves for lunch.

3 medium-size avocados, chopped

1 tablespoon (15 ml) lime juice

2 teaspoons unsalted curry powder

1 teaspoon sea salt

1 clove garlic, crushed

Dash of cayenne pepper (optional)

2 Roma tomatoes, seeded and diced

¼ cup (40 g) diced red onion

2 Medjool dates, diced

2 tablespoons (2 g) chopped cilantro

1. Place the avocados, lime juice, curry powder, sea salt, garlic, and cayenne in a medium-size bowl and mash with a fork.

2. Add the tomatoes, red onion, dates, and cilantro and combine gently.

3. Adjust the flavors if you prefer more salt, sweet, or spice. Serve with flax chips or celery sticks or add a scoop onto a salad.

To store, lay a piece of plastic wrap so it sits right on the guacamole, eliminating all air exposure. It is also helpful to keep an avocado pit in the dip for freshness.

The guacamole will keep in the refrigerator for 2 days.

VARIATION: For a classic guacamole omit the curry powder and dates.

NUTRITION NOTE: High in heart-healthy, monounsaturated fats, avocados have been shown to lower cholesterol and protect against strokes. They also contain the antioxidants glutathione and vitamin E and the phytonutrient lutein, which has been linked to eye health and the prevention of macular degeneration and cataracts. Avocados are also great for the skin when applied as a mask, but I'd much rather eat them.

Entrées

For the days I crave something hearty and familiar, these are my go-to recipes. Some take a little bit of planning ahead, but they're well worth the extra effort. For the ultra busy, I included some shortcuts to help you lessen your prep time.

South-of-the-Border Soft Tacos

Makes 6 servings

TORTILLAS
Prep time: 15 minutes
Drying time: 5 to 6 hours

TACO MEAT
Prep time: 30 minutes
Drying time: 1½ to 2½ hours

GUACAMOLE
Prep time: 5 minutes

There's no reason you can't have your own Mexican fiesta when you go raw. These tacos are packed full of southwestern flavor without leaving you weighed down or bloated. Make the components a day or two ahead of time and bring to room temperature or warm them in the dehydrator before assembling. Serve with Mexican Wild Rice (see page 98).

CORN TORTILLAS

4 cups (600 g) chopped yellow or red bell peppers

2 cups (300 g) fresh or frozen corn, thawed

2 tablespoons (30 ml) lime juice

½ teaspoon sea salt

1 small avocado

2 tablespoons psyllium husk powder

TORTILLAS

1. Process the bell peppers, corn, lime juice, and salt in a high-power blender. Use the tamper or a spatula to keep the blades moving if needed. While the blender is running, add the avocado and psyllium powder and blend until smooth.

2. Spread ⅓ cup (80 ml) of the batter onto a nonstick dehydrator sheet (a), 4 on a sheet.

3. Use a small offset spatula to spread into 5-inch (13-cm) disks (b). The batter will yield about 12 tortillas.

4. Dry at 110°F (43°C) for 4 hours or until dry enough to peel from the sheet without sticking (c), transfer to a mesh screen, and dry for an additional 1 to 2 hours. The tortillas should be dry but still pliable. If they are too dry, lightly spray both sides with water.

recipe continues...

MEXICAN SEASONED VEGGIE MEAT

2 cups (290 g) Brazil nuts, un-soaked

4 cups (496 g) finely diced zucchini

1⅓ cups (93 g) minced white or cremini mushrooms

½ cup (80 g) minced onion

½ cup (60 g) minced celery

½ cup (60 g) Mexican chili powder

¼ cup (60 ml) lemon juice

1 to 2 teaspoons sea salt, less if using salted chili powder

2 cloves garlic, minced

½ teaspoon cayenne pepper

SIMPLE GUACAMOLE

2 avocados, cubed

1 teaspoon lemon juice

¼ teaspoon sea salt

ADDITIONAL FILLING

3 cups (115 g) shredded lettuce or cabbage

Pico de Gallo (see page 169)

Sour Cream (see page 169)

VEGGIE MEAT

1. Place the Brazil nuts in a food processor and grind into a flour.

2. In a large bowl, combine the Brazil nut flour with the zucchini, mushrooms, onion, celery, chili powder, lemon juice, salt, garlic, and cayenne.

3. Spread the mixture onto 2 dehydrator trays lined with nonstick sheets (see photo at right) and dry at 110°F (43°C) for 1½ hours. Transfer to mesh dehydrator sheets for another hour. Do not overdry.

GUACAMOLE

Mash all the ingredients in a bowl with a fork until creamy. Add more salt or lemon juice if desired.

ASSEMBLY

1. For warm rice and veggie meat, place in the dehydrator for 30 to 60 minutes at 145°F (63°C) before assembling.

2. Fill each tortilla with meat and top with lettuce, guacamole, pico de gallo, and sour cream.

Chef's Tip: Feel free to use cabbage or romaine leaves as tortilla shells. You can also buy premade guacamole and pico de gallo, though I think fresh always tastes best!

a   b   c

Garden of Eden Pesto Wrap

Makes 4 servings
Prep time: 45 minutes
Drying time: 6 to 7 hours

These veggie wrappers are great to keep on hand when you want to fix something fast and portable. I like to fill mine with lettuce, tomato, avocado, and sprouts, but you can also use carrots, cucumbers, zucchini, and olives. Zucchini Hummus (see page 97) also tastes really great in place of the pesto.

VEGGIE WRAPPER

6 cups (900 g) seeded, chopped red bell peppers

4 cups (720 g) chopped tomatoes

1 teaspoon sea salt

1 small avocado

2 tablespoons (16 g) psyllium husk powder

WRAPPERS

1. Place the bell peppers, tomatoes, and sea salt into a high-power blender and process until smooth. Use a tamper or a spatula to get the blades moving. While blending, add the avocado, followed by the psyllium husk powder.

2. Divide the mixture among 4 dehydrator trays lined with nonstick sheets, about 1½ cups (355 ml) per tray.

3. Use an offset spatula to evenly spread into large disks (a), making sure there are no thin or thick spots. The center often ends up being thicker than the edges, so be mindful as you spread it so the wrapper dries evenly.

NOTE: You can make smaller, taco-size wraps if you prefer. Make four 6-inch (15-cm) wraps per tray.

4. Dry at 110°F (43°C) for 5 or more hours. As soon as they are dry enough to peel off the nonstick sheet without sticking, transfer to a mesh dehydrator screen and dry for another 1 to 2 hours until dry but still pliable. If you overdry them, spray both sides lightly with water to soften.

recipe continues...

a

PESTO SPREAD

1 cup (40 g) packed basil

½ cup (70 g) pine nuts

¼ cup (60 ml) olive oil

1 clove garlic

1 teaspoon lemon juice

¼ teaspoon sea salt

FILLING

8 romaine or red leaf lettuce leaves

2 tomatoes, sliced

2 avocados, sliced

2 cups (100 g) broccoli sprouts or your favorite sprouts

1 bell pepper, cut into strips

¼ small red onion, sliced

PESTO SPREAD

Place all the ingredients into a food processor and blend until smooth. Scrape down the sides with a spatula as needed.

ASSEMBLY

1. Spread the pesto over the bottom center of the wrap (a).
2. Layer the lettuce, tomato, avocado, sprouts, bell pepper, and onion over the pesto sauce (b).
3. Fold two ends of the wrap toward the center (c), and then roll the end closest to you (d), tucking the filling in as you roll (e, f, g & h).
4. Turn over so seam is on the bottom and slice in half.

Store the wrappers by themselves by rolling them into a cylinder and wrapping with plastic wrap so they don't dry out. Wrappers will keep for 2 weeks in the refrigerator. Pesto will keep for 3 days.

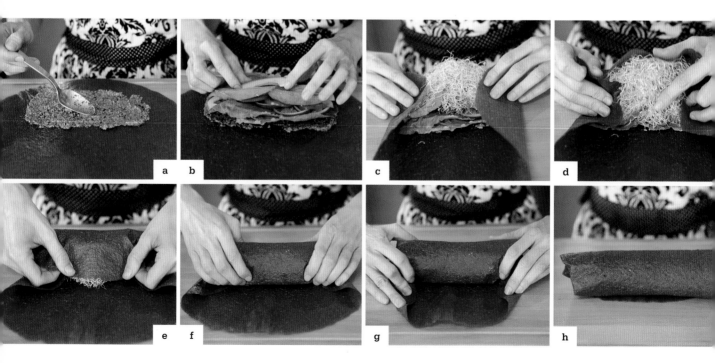

WRAP VARIATION : COLLARD LEAVES

Chef's Tip: Collard leaves make great wrappers as well.

1. Take a large collard leaf and remove the bottom stem with a knife (a).
2. Carefully fillet the thickest part of the stem so that your leaf is pliable (b).
3. Place your filling in the bottom center of the leaf (c & d).
4. Fold the sides toward the center and then roll from the bottom up, tucking in the filling and sides as needed to make a tight wrap (e, f, g, & h)

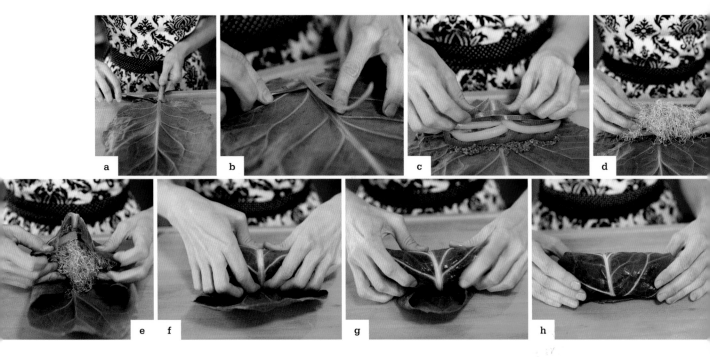

a   b   c   d

e   f   g   h

Broccoli and Mushrooms with Wild Rice

Makes 4 servings
Prep time: 30 minutes

This hearty, tangy, sweet, and savory dish was inspired by Lisa Viger's food blog. I highly recommend checking out her website, www.rawon10.blogspot.com, if you are in need of some modestly priced culinary inspiration. This dish can be made with or without rice. Just add 1 cup (70 g) more of both the broccoli and the mushrooms if omitting the rice. You can also substitute balsamic vinegar for lemon juice to make it truly raw.

Optional Tip: Before cutting into florets, dip the head of broccoli into hot water for 5 seconds to bring out the brilliant green color and make it more palatable for children.

½ cup (120 ml) olive oil

½ cup (120 ml) balsamic vinegar

2 tablespoons (40 g) liquid honey or agave nectar

2 cloves garlic, crushed

1½ teaspoons sea salt

1 teaspoon freshly ground pepper

6 cups (426 g) broccoli florets

2 cups (330 g) bloomed wild rice (see page 44)

1 cup (160 g) diced onion

3 cups (210 g) sliced cremini or baby portobello mushrooms

1. Whisk together the oil, vinegar, honey, garlic, salt, and pepper in a small bowl.

2. In a large bowl, toss the broccoli, wild rice, and onion together with the sauce. Add the mushrooms and toss again until thoroughly coated. This is to keep the mushrooms from absorbing all of the sauce too quickly.

3. Serve immediately, or if you prefer to give it a cooked feel, allow to marinate for 1 to 2 hours at room temperature or place the covered bowl in a dehydrator at 145°F (63°C) for 30 to 60 minutes.

The dish will keep for 3 days in the refrigerator.

NUTRITION NOTE: Broccoli is a great source of vitamin C, calcium, fiber, and protein. Use the leftover broccoli stalks for your green juice or shred it and add it to your salads for extra fiber.

Spaghetti Bolognese

Makes 4 to 6 servings
Soak time: 2 hours
Prep time: 1 hour

An Italian classic without the food coma. Serve this to your raw food naysayers and watch them change their tune.

SAUCE

1½ cups (84 g) sun-dried tomatoes, soaked 1–2 hours, drained

1½ cups (270 g) seeded, chopped tomatoes (2 or 3)

¼ cup (60 ml) olive oil

2 tablespoons (5 g) fresh basil or 2 teaspoons dried

2 tablespoons (8 g) fresh oregano or 2 teaspoons dried

2 cloves garlic

1 teaspoon sea salt

¼ teaspoon crushed red pepper

Dash of freshly ground pepper

1 recipe Ground Veggie Meat (see page 96)

NOODLES

6 medium-size zucchini or yellow summer squash, peeled

SAUCE

1. Place all the ingredients into a blender and process until smooth.
2. Transfer to a medium-sized bowl and gently fold the veggie meat into the tomato sauce.

OPTIONAL: Place the sauce in a dehydrator at 145°F (63°C) for 1 hour or warm in a saucepan over very low heat.

NOODLES

1. Use a spiralizer to create noodles from the zucchini (see page 40).
2. Gently toss the noodles with the sauce and serve immediately.

Stored separately, the sauce and veggie meat will keep for 1 week in the refrigerator.

Chef's Tip: If you don't have time to make veggie meat, top your spaghetti with some minced portobello mushrooms to make it heartier.

NUTRITION NOTE: Sun-dried tomatoes are a great source of lycopene that becomes even more bioavailable when we process them in a high-power blender. Lycopene has antioxidant properties shown to be effective in preventing prostate cancer as well as increasing fertility in men. Eating large amounts of lycopene can also create internal SPF that helps reduce UV skin damage.

Vegetable Maki Sushi

Makes 6 servings
Prep time: 40 minutes

These fresh, crunchy rolls are as much fun to make as they are to eat.

SESAME-GINGER DIPPING SAUCE

¼ cup (60 ml) tamari

2 tablespoons (30 ml) brown rice vinegar

2 teaspoons agave nectar

½ teaspoon grated ginger

½ teaspoon sesame seeds

MAKI SUSHI

3 cups (390 g) chopped jicama

6 sheets untoasted nori

1 cucumber, peeled, seeded, and cut into sticks

1 red bell pepper, cut into thin strips

2 avocados, sliced

2 cups (100 g) alfalfa or other similar sprouts

DIPPING SAUCE

Whisk all the ingredients together in a small bowl.

MAKI SUSHI

1. Place the jicama into a food processor and pulse until it turns into rice-size pieces. Do not overprocess; you don't want mush. Lay the jicama rice on a clean towel and roll it tightly to soak up excess moisture.

2. To assemble, place 1 nori sheet on a sushi mat vertically with the shiny side down.

3. Spread a thin layer of jicama rice on the bottom half of the sheet (a).

4. Layer a few cucumber sticks, bell pepper strips, avocado slices, and sprouts over the jicama rice (b & c).

5. Use your sushi mat to gently begin the roll, using your fingertips to tuck in the filling as you go (d & e).

6. As soon as it becomes a solid cylinder, remove the sushi mat and use your hands to continue rolling tightly (f). You can also do this process without the sushi mat entirely.

7. Moisten the edge of the nori sheet with water to seal (g).

8. Use a sharp knife to slice into 6 to 8 pieces (h).

9. Serve with the dipping sauce.

The dipping sauce will keep for 1 week in refrigerator, while the jicama rice will keep 3 or 4 days.

HEALTH NOTE: Nori is high in protein and iron and rich in essential thyroid-supporting iodine.

a b c d

e   f   g   h

Asian Noodle "Stir-Fry"

Makes 4 servings
Soak time: 30 minutes
Prep time: 30 minutes
Marinate: 1 hour

For a "stir-fry" this is incredibly light yet still filling and a favorite among my friends because of its wonderful array of Asian flavors.

NOODLES

1 package (12 ounces, or 340 g) kelp noodles

Juice of 1 small lemon

½ cup (40 g) arame, soaked 5 minutes

2 cups (60 g) packed baby spinach

2 cups (140 g) shredded napa cabbage

1 cup (70 g) thinly sliced shiitake mushrooms

½ cup (25 g) bean sprouts

2 scallions, green and white parts, thinly sliced

1 large carrot, julienned

1 tablespoon (8 g) black sesame seeds

SAUCE

⅓ cup (80 ml) tamari

3 tablespoons (25 g) palm sugar

1 tablespoon (8 g) grated ginger

1 tablespoon (15 ml) toasted sesame oil

1 teaspoon sea salt

1 clove garlic, crushed or finely minced

½ teaspoon crushed red pepper

¼ cup (28 g) chopped almonds

NOODLES

1. Loosen and rinse the kelp noodles. Place in a medium-size bowl and cover with water. Add the lemon juice and allow to soak for at least 30 minutes. This will soften the noodles.

2. Rinse and drain well and transfer to a large bowl.

3. Add the soaked arame, spinach, cabbage, mushrooms, bean sprouts, scallion, carrot, and sesame seeds and toss.

SAUCE

1. Combine the tamari, palm sugar, ginger, sesame oil, salt, garlic, and crushed red pepper in a blender. Pour the sauce over the noodles and toss.

2. Let sit for 1 hour to allow the flavors to mingle. You may even place it in your dehydrator for 1 hour at 145°F (63°C) for a warm noodle dish.

3. Top each serving with the chopped almonds.

This dish will keep for 1 day in the refrigerator.

Chef's Note: Kelp noodles are what remains when the outer skin of kelp is removed. They are indeed raw and make a great alternative to flour noodles. They're neutral tasting and will take on whatever flavor or sauce you dress them in.

Classic Veggie Pizza

Makes 8 servings

PIZZA CRUST	SAUCE	CHEESE	MARINATED MUSHROOMS
Prep time: 15 minutes Drying time: 4 hours	Soak time: 1 to 2 hours Prep time: 10 minutes	Soak time: 2 hours Prep time: 10 minutes	Prep time: 20 minutes

I have to thank the very creative raw food chef May Salem for inspiring this pizza recipe. While pregnant with her first child, May went on a pizza-making mission and came up with the best sprouted pizza I have ever had. Don't be overwhelmed by the directions; it is so worth the effort. I recommend doubling the recipe and making your crusts in advance. The rest of it takes little time to put together. You can substitute spelt or if you're gluten sensitive, buckwheat, in place of the kamut.

PIZZA CRUST

2½ cups (478 g) (1 cup [186 g] dry) sprouted kamut (see page 51)

½ teaspoon sea salt

½ cup (120 ml) water

2 tablespoons (30 ml) olive oil

1½ cups (112 g) ground golden flaxseeds

1. Place the sprouted grain and salt in a food processor and blend until it breaks down, scraping down the sides of the container as needed (a).

2. Add the water and olive oil while processing and continue to blend until it becomes doughy.

3. Transfer to a mixing bowl and add the ground flaxseeds (b). Mix well using a spatula or dampened hands (c). Knead until thoroughly mixed.

4. Pour a small amount of olive oil onto a nonstick dehydrator sheet (d). Take a rolling pin and spread the oil over the sheet evenly (e). Using your hands (f) and the rolling pin (g), press the dough into a ¼-inch-thick (6 mm) round or square pizza crust. Curl in the edges if you would like it to look like a traditional pizza crust (h & i).

5. Dry for 2 hours at 110°F (38°C) and then flip onto a mesh screen for an additional 2 hours. It should be dry but still slightly pliable.

Dried crusts may be stored in the refrigerator for 5 days. It is best to cover them in plastic wrap to keep them from drying out.

recipe continues...

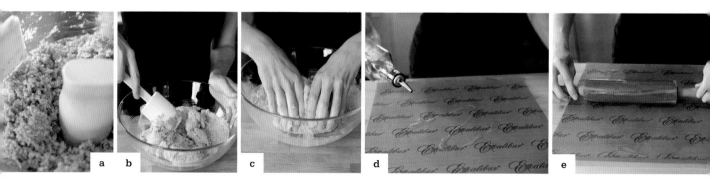

a   b   c   d   e

PIZZA SAUCE

1 cup (56 g) sun-dried tomatoes, soaked 1–2 hours, drained, soak water reserved

1 medium-size tomato, seeded and chopped

1 tablespoon (15 ml) lemon juice

1 tablespoon (15 ml) olive oil

1 clove garlic (optional)

1 medium-size date

1 teaspoon fresh oregano

1 teaspoon fresh basil

1 teaspoon fresh thyme

¼ teaspoon sea salt

Pinch of crushed red pepper flakes

CHEESE

1 cup (120 g) cashews, soaked 2 hours

¼ cup (60 ml) water

2 tablespoons (24 g) nutritional yeast

1 tablespoon (15 ml) lemon juice

¼ teaspoon sea salt

MARINATED MUSHROOMS

¾ cup (53 g) chopped white mushrooms

⅓ cup (55 g) diced onion

1 clove garlic, minced

2 tablespoons (30 ml) tamari

1 tablespoon (15 ml) olive oil

TOPPINGS

1½ cups (45 g) chopped spinach

1 small red bell pepper, sliced or chopped

¼ cup (25 g) dried olives, pitted and sliced

Parmesan Cheese (optional; see page 169)

SAUCE

Place all the ingredients in a blender and process until smooth. Add the soak water from the sun-dried tomatoes, 1 tablespoon (15 ml) at a time, to thin the sauce if needed.

CHEESE

Process all the ingredients in a blender until smooth.

MUSHROOMS

Place all the ingredients in a small jar or container and shake well. Let sit for 15 minutes.

ASSEMBLY

1. Spread the sun-dried tomato sauce over the pizza crust (j).
2. Use a spoon to drop small dollops of cheese over the sauce. Use an offset spatula to spread the cheese evenly (k). It does not need to be perfectly even. I like to see the sauce peek through.
3. Top the pizza with the spinach, red bell pepper, olives, and marinated mushrooms (l & m).
4. Place on a mesh dehydrator sheet and dry at 110°F (46°C) for 3 hours.

BBQ Veggie Burgers

Makes 6 burgers

BURGER PATTY
Prep time: 30 minutes
Drying time: 5 hours

BUN
Prep time: 30 minutes
Drying time: 5 to 6 hours

Another hearty, classic dish made raw and super nutritious.

VEGGIE BURGERS

1½ cups (218 g) almonds, soaked 8–12 hours and dehydrated for 8 hours, or until completely dry

¾ cup (113 g) diced red bell pepper

¾ cup (120 g) diced white or yellow onion

¾ cup (90 g) diced celery

1 clove garlic, crushed

2 tablespoons (8 g) fresh parsley, or 2 teaspoons dried

3 tablespoons (45 ml) tamari

¼ teaspoon black pepper

1 cup (112 g) ground flaxseeds

BUN

2 cups (382 g) sprouted kamut (see page 51)

Pinch of sea salt

2 tablespoons (30 ml) olive oil

⅓ cup (80 ml) water

1¼ cups (142 g) ground golden flaxseeds

½ teaspoon black sesame seeds

FILLINGS

Sliced onions

Sliced tomatoes

Lettuce

Alfalfa sprouts

BBQ Sauce (see page 168)

VEGGIE BURGERS

1. Place the almonds into a food processor and grind into a flour (a).
2. Add the bell pepper, onion, celery, garlic, parsley, tamari, and black pepper and pulse several times until well incorporated (b). Leave some chunks of vegetable visible.
3. Transfer to a bowl and stir in the ground flaxseeds (c).
4. Shape into six 3½-inch (8.5-cm) patties (about ½ cup [115 g] of mixture each), and place onto a mesh dehydrator tray (d, e & f).
5. Dry at 110°F (43°C) for 5 hours.

BUN

(See pizza dough instructions, page 119 for photos.)

1. Place the sprouted kamut and salt into a food processor and process until the seeds break down. Use a spatula to scrape down the sides as needed.
2. Add the olive oil and water and blend again.
3. Transfer to a mixing bowl and knead in the flaxseeds with your hands or a spatula until you have a dough.
4. Lightly oil your hands with olive oil and shape the dough into 12 flat disks, a little less than ¼ cup [60 g] each.
5. Lay the disks on a lightly oiled nonstick dehydrator sheet. Sprinkle sesame seeds onto half of the disks and press gently into the dough (g).

a

b

c

6. Dry at 110°F (43°C) for 3 hours. Flip onto a mesh dehydrator tray and dry for an additional 2 to 3 hours. They should be dry on the outside but still moist to the touch.

Serve with sliced onions, tomatoes, lettuce, sprouts, and BBQ Sauce.

Chef's Tip: You can skip the bun and just wrap your burger in lettuce leaves. Napa cabbage makes a particularly good wrapper. If you don't have time to make BBQ sauce you can substitute it with store-bought, natural, organic condiments.

d e   f   g

Coconut-Curry Samosas with Plum Chutney

Makes 4 to 6 servings
Prep time: 1 hour
Drying time: 5 hours

In India, traditional curries are composed of twenty or more spices and can range from mild to very spicy. Look for one that is unsalted and contains spices that you like. Outside of the supermarket shelves there are probably as many curries as there are stars in the sky. Visit gourmet or ethnic food markets for a truly flavorful blend.

SAMOSA WRAPPERS

2½ cups (200 g) young Thai coconut meat

1 teaspoon or more turmeric (for color)

¼ teaspoon sea salt

FILLING

1 cup (30 g) packed spinach

2 teaspoons olive oil

⅛ plus ½ teaspoon sea salt

2 cups (330 g) bloomed wild rice (see page 44)

2 tablespoons (15 g) chopped cashews

1 tablespoon (6.3 g) unsalted curry powder, or more to taste

2 tablespoons (20 g) minced white onion

SAMOSA WRAPPERS

1. Process the ingredients in a high-power blender until smooth and creamy. Use the tamper or a spatula (watch the blades!) to help keep things moving.
2. Divide between 2 dehydrator trays lined with nonstick sheets.
3. Use an offset spatula to spread the batter evenly over the entire sheet, leaving a small border. It doesn't have to be perfect, but try to avoid any thin spots (a, b & c).
4. Dry at 110°F (43°C) for 4 hours or until completely dry on one side. You should be able to gently peel the wrapper without it sticking.
5. Remove the wrapper from the nonstick sheet and dry for an additional hour or until dry but still pliable (d). If too dry, lightly spray with water to soften.
6. Trim the edges with a knife and slice each sheet into 4 even strips (e, f & g).

FILLING

1. Combine the spinach, olive oil, and the ⅛ teaspoon sea salt in a bowl and allow to marinate for 15 minutes to soften.
2. Combine the rice, cashews, curry powder, remaining ½ teaspoon salt, and onion in a bowl. Add more curry as needed. When the spinach is wilted, fold into the rice mixture.

recipe continues...

e   f   g

PLUM CHUTNEY

¾ cup (131 g) dried plums, soaked 30 minutes

⅓ cup (80 ml) water

1 tablespoon (15 ml) tamari

1 tablespoon (10 g) diced white or yellow onion

1 tablespoon (20 g) agave nectar

1 tablespoon (15 ml) apple cider vinegar

¼ teaspoon ground mustard

CHUTNEY

Place all the ingredients in a food processor and blend until well incorporated but still a little chunky.

ASSEMBLY

1. Take a samosa strip and fold one end into a triangle (h).
2. Continue to fold this way until you create a cone or pocket (i, j & k).
3. Fill with as much rice filling as it can hold and continue to fold the wrapper until you reach the end (l, m & n).
4. Trim the excess wrapper with a knife (o).
5. Seal with water (p & q).

Serve with the plum chutney. This dish will keep for 4 days in the refrigerator.

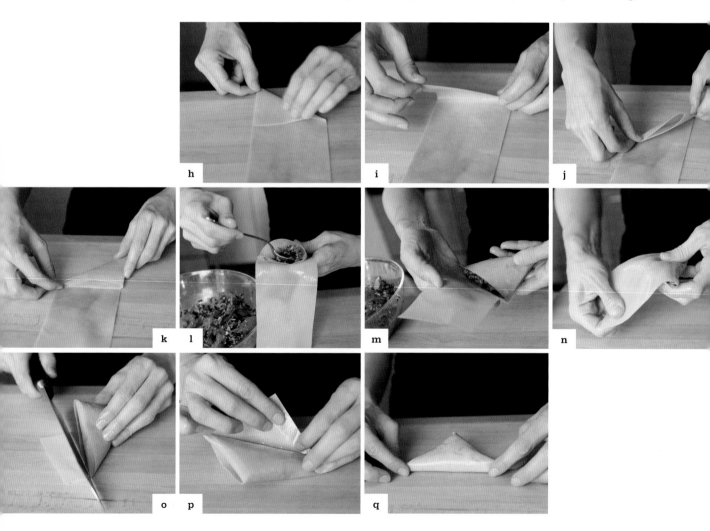

Vegetarian Homestyle Chili

Makes 4 to 6 servings
Soak time: 1 to 2 hours
Prep time: 40 minutes

This is true southern comfort, raw style. I actually like this better the next day when the vegetables soften and the flavors have had time to mingle. Chili is really only as good as the chili powder you use, so look for a good brand at gourmet grocery stores, or if you're really adventurous, make your own. Serve with Sour Cream (see page 169).

SAUCE

½ cup (27 g) sun-dried tomatoes, soaked 1–2 hours in 2 cups (475 ml) water, soak water reserved

1½ cups (355 ml) soak water from sun-dried tomatoes

2 Roma tomatoes, seeded and chopped

1 tablespoon (20 g) honey or agave nectar

1 tablespoon (15 ml) olive oil

3 tablespoons (24 g) unsalted chili powder

2 tablespoons (20 g) chopped white or yellow onion

1½ teaspoons sea salt

1 tablespoon (4 g) fresh oregano or 1 teaspoon dried

½ teaspoon cumin

⅛ teaspoon cayenne pepper

CHILI

2 cups Ground Veggie Meat (see page 96)

1¾ cups (198 g) zucchini sliced into half-moons

1¾ cups (315 g) seeded and chopped tomatoes

⅓ cup (50 g) fresh corn kernels

⅓ cup (55 g) diced white or yellow onion

1 jalapeño pepper, seeded and diced

SAUCE

Place all the ingredients into a blender and process until well mixed. Adjust the salt and spices if needed.

CHILI

1. Place all the ingredients into a mixing bowl and combine with the sauce.

2. Serve immediately, or for a warm chili, place in a dehydrator at 145°F (63°C) for 1 hour. Spoon out the excess moisture.

The chili will keep for 3 days in the refrigerator.

Creamy Tomato Fettuccine

Makes 4 to 6 servings
Soak time: 2 hours
Prep time: 35 minutes

No carbohydrate overload for this Italian "pasta" dish. I've served this to friends who didn't even realize it was raw. It contains all the elements I love about Italian food: garlic, olive oil, basil, oregano, crushed red pepper, and tomatoes all in a creamy sauce. That's *amore*!

SAUCE

¾ cup (90 g) cashews, soaked 2 hours

¾ cup (175 ml) water

3 tablespoons (21 g) sun-dried tomato powder*

1½ tablespoons (6 g) fresh oregano or 1½ teaspoons dried

1½ tablespoons (4 g) fresh basil or 1½ teaspoons dried

1 tablespoon (15 ml) lemon juice

1 tablespoon (15 ml) olive oil

1 tablespoon (20 g) agave nectar

1 clove garlic

1½ teaspoons sea salt

¼ teaspoon crushed red pepper (optional)

NOODLES

6 medium-size zucchini, peeled

GARNISHES

3 tomatoes, diced

2 tablespoons (7 g) finely chopped thyme

Freshly ground pepper to taste (optional)

SAUCE

Process all the ingredients in a blender until very smooth.

NOODLES

Use a mandoline to slice the zucchini into long, flat strips (a). Stack the strips, and with a knife slice the zucchini into fettuccine-like ribbons (b).

ASSEMBLY

In a large bowl, very gently combine the sauce and noodles, using only enough sauce to coat the noodles. You may have extra sauce left over. Garnish with the diced tomatoes, finely chopped thyme, and freshly ground pepper.

Chef's Tips: If using a high-power blender, blend the sauce until it heats up, or you may warm the sauce on your stovetop at very low heat and serve over room-temperature noodles. It is best not to combine the noodles and the sauce until you are ready to serve them; otherwise, the dish can become watery.

Stored separately, the sauce will keep for 1 week in the refrigerator, and the noodles will keep for 2 days.

NUTRITION NOTE: Zucchini is high in heart-healthy potassium and container vitamins A and C and the phytonutrients lutein and zeaxanthin, two members of the carotenoid family responsible for protecting our eyes from macular degeneration.

*To make sun-dried tomato powder, process dried tomatoes in a spice grinder or coffee grinder until it becomes a fine powder.

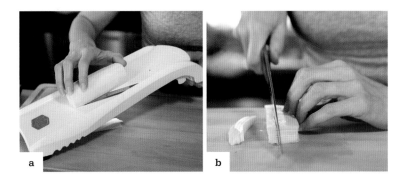

a   b

Desserts

When I first started teaching raw food classes I would promote them by giving out samples of my raw fudge brownies. I admit this was a bit like dealing crack but at least my classes sold out and were full of students eager to learn more about raw foods.

Ask any raw foodist how they got hooked on raw and they'll tell you it was the desserts. Just be mindful when indulging that because they are denser and richer than other desserts, you will be satiated with a much smaller serving.

Orange-Chocolate Mousse Parfait

Makes 8 servings
Soak time: 2 hours
Prep time: 30 minutes
Chill time: 2 hours

Don't tell people that the secret ingredient is avocado until they try this dreamy, decadent dessert.

MOUSSE

2 large avocados, or more as needed

²/₃ cup (53 g) cacao powder

¾ cup (255 g) agave nectar

1½ teaspoons grated orange zest

VANILLA CREAM

1½ cups (180 g) cashews, soaked 2 hours

¹/₃ cup (80 ml) coconut oil, warmed to liquid

¹/₃ cup (80 ml) water

¹/₃ cup (115 g) agave nectar

1 teaspoon vanilla extract

MOUSSE

Place all the ingredients in a food processor and blend for 1 to 2 minutes until smooth, with the consistency of a thick pudding. Add more avocado if too thin. Scrape down the sides of the container with a spatula as needed.

VANILLA CREAM

1. Place the cashews, coconut oil, water, agave nectar, and vanilla into a high-power blender and process until very smooth.
2. Chill the mousse and cream for 2 hours or until firm, then layer into parfait glasses using a pastry bag or a spoon.

Stored separately, the mousse will keep for 3 days in the refrigerator and the cream will keep for 1 week.

Fresh Summer Fruit Tart

Makes 8 servings
Soak time: 2 hours
Prep time: 45 minutes
Chill time: 2 hours

This pretty dessert is always a hit at tea parties, showers, or even Mother's Day brunch.

CRUST

2 cups (270 g) macadamia nuts

Pinch of sea salt (optional)

⅓ cup (48 g) Medjool dates

CUSTARD

1 cup (120 g) cashews, soaked 2 hours

⅔ cup (160 ml) coconut oil, warmed to liquid

½ vanilla bean, scraped

¼ cup (85 g) agave nectar

2 tablespoons (30 ml) water

FRUIT TOPPING

1 cup (170 g) quartered strawberries

¾ cup (109 g) blueberries

2 kiwis, peeled and sliced

Fresh mint for garnish

CRUST

1. Place the macadamia nuts and sea salt into a food processor and process until ground. Add the dates and process again until incorporated. Don't overprocess, or it will release too much oil.

2. Spread the mixture evenly into a 9½-inch (24-cm) removable-bottom tart pan lined with parchment paper.

3. Starting in the center, press with your fingers to form a firm crust (a). Make sure the sides are firm so they don't lose their shape when removed from the tart pan (b).

CUSTARD

1. Process the cashews, coconut oil, vanilla bean, agave nectar, and water in a high-power blender until very smooth.

2. Pour the custard over the crust and smooth with an offset spatula (c & d). Chill for at least 2 hours.

Before serving, top the custard with the sliced strawberries, blueberries, and kiwis. Garnish with fresh mint.

This dish will keep for 2 days in the refrigerator.

Chef's Tip: Use whatever fruit is in season. Fall is a great time to make a cinnamon apple/pear tart, while in the winter months you can create an orange and pomegranate fruit tart.

a b   c   d

Mexican Spiced Brownies

Makes 12 to 16 servings
Prep time: 30 minutes
Chill time: 1 to 2 hours

I love spicy chocolate, so I made this version with a bit of a kick. If you prefer less heat, cut the cayenne by half. To make it kid-friendly, omit the cayenne.

BROWNIE BASE

4 cups (400 g) walnuts, soaked 6–8 hours and dehydrated

⅔ cup (100 g) raisins

⅔ cup (97 g) Medjool dates

⅔ cup (53 g) cacao powder

1 tablespoon (7 g) Mexican (Ceylon) cinnamon

2 teaspoons vanilla extract

2 teaspoons finely ground star anise

2 teaspoons cayenne pepper

Pinch of sea salt (optional)

2 tablespoons (30 ml) water

FROSTING

½ cup (170 g) maple syrup or agave nectar

¼ cup (60 ml) coconut oil, warmed to liquid

⅔ cup (53 g) cacao powder

BROWNIE BASE

1. Place the walnuts into a food processor and grind to the consistency of a meal (a). Don't overprocess, or it will release too much oil.
2. Add the raisins and dates and process until the mixture is well combined (b).
3. Add the cacao powder, cinnamon, vanilla, star anise, cayenne, and sea salt and process again until the mixture is sticky yet still crumbly (c). Transfer to a large mixing bowl.
4. Add the water and mix well, using your hands. It should start to resemble a dough (d).
5. Spread the mixture evenly into an 8 x 8-inch (20 x 20-cm) baking pan (e) lined with parchment paper and press firmly with your hands (f).

FROSTING

1. Add the maple syrup to a blender first, followed by the coconut oil and cacao powder. Blend well until smooth (g).
2. Spread the topping over the brownies and chill for at least 1 to 2 hours (h).
3. Remove the brownie by lifting up the parchment paper (i) and slice into 12 to 16 pieces.

Store in the refrigerator for up to 1 week or in the freezer for 1 month.

Chef's Tip: Try substituting cayenne pepper with chipotle or ancho pepper for a whole new experience. Chipotle is smoky and spicy, while ancho is mild and sweet. For a traditional brownie, omit the cayenne, anise, and cinnamon.

a   b   c   d   e

a   b   c

Apple Cobbler with Maple Cream

Makes 8 servings
Soak time: 2 hours
Prep time: 35 minutes
Warming time: 1 hour

An apple a day keeps the doctor away, and what better way to get your daily apple than with this traditional autumn dessert? It is perfectly sweet and gooey, and incredible when served warm. It is made even more delicious with a scoop of Basic Vanilla Bean Ice Cream (see page 139).

TOPPING/CRUST

1 cup (100 g) pecans or walnuts, soaked and dehydrated (see page 47 for soak times)

¼ cup (30 g) palm sugar or evaporated cane sugar

¼ cup (35 g) raisins

¼ cup (36 g) Medjool dates

⅛ teaspoon sea salt

½ cup (40 g) rolled oats

FILLING

2 tablespoons (40 g) agave nectar

1½ tablespoons (25 ml) lemon juice

¼ teaspoon pumpkin pie spice

3 cups (330 g) (2 to 3 large) apples, peeled, cored, and thinly sliced

MAPLE CREAM

1 cup (120 g) cashews, soaked 2 hours

½ cup (170 g) maple syrup

¼ cup (60 ml) water

½ vanilla bean, scraped

TOPPING

In a food processor, combine the pecans with the palm sugar and process until you get a coarse meal. Add the raisins, dates, and salt and process until the mixture sticks together. Be careful not to overprocess, or it will become too oily. In a medium-size bowl combine the topping mixture with the rolled oats.

FILLING

In a small bowl, combine the agave nectar, lemon juice, and pumpkin pie spice. In a large mixing bowl, toss the apples with the agave mixture.

MAPLE CREAM

Process the cashews, maple syrup, water, and vanilla bean until very smooth, about 2 minutes in a high-power blender. Store in a large squeeze bottle for easy use or in an airtight container.

ASSEMBLY

1. Sprinkle half of the nut mixture in the bottom of a 9-inch (23-cm) round pie dish or 1-quart (946-ml) baking dish (a).
2. Layer with the apple filling and then sprinkle with the remaining topping (b & c).
3. Warm in the dehydrator at 145°F (63°C) for 1 hour and top each serving with the maple cream.

Store the apple cobbler and maple cream in the refrigerator. The cobbler will keep for 3 or 4 days, and the maple cream will keep for 2 weeks.

NUTRITION NOTE: Apples are surprisingly high in antioxidants and have a long list of health benefits. Studies show they may be able to reduce the risk of tumors, asthma, diabetes, and osteoporosis.

Delicious Ice Cream Recipes

Basic Vanilla Bean Ice Cream

Makes 4 cups (506 g)
Soak time: 2 hours
Prep time: 25 minutes
Chill time: 2 hours

This is the perfect topping for warm Apple Cobbler (see page 137), or play around and mix in some nuts, raw chocolate shavings, or Ice Box Chocolate Chip Cookie (see page 141) bits just before freezing.

1 cup (120 g) cashews, soaked 2 hours

1¼ cups (295 ml) water

¾ cup (60 g) young Thai coconut meat

1 vanilla bean, scraped

2 tablespoons (30 ml) alcohol-free vanilla extract

½ cup (170 g) agave nectar

1 tablespoon (7.5 g) lecithin powder

Pinch of sea salt (optional)

⅓ cup (80 ml) coconut oil, warmed to liquid

1. Place the cashews, water, coconut meat, vanilla bean, vanilla extract, agave, lecithin, and salt into a high-power blender and process until very smooth.
2. Add the coconut oil and blend again.
3. Chill the mixture and then process in an ice cream maker according to the manufacturer's instructions.
4. Fold in any additions and then place in the freezer to firm.

Chef's Tip: Your mixture may taste overly sweet after blending, but the sweetness will decrease once it's frozen.

Strawberry Ice Cream

Makes 4 cups (506 g)
Soak time: 2 hours
Prep time: 25 minutes
Chill time: 2 hours

2 cups (340 g) chopped strawberries

¾ cup (90 g) cashews, soaked 2 hours

¾ cup (175 ml) water

⅔ cup (53 g) young Thai coconut meat

½ cup (170 g) agave nectar

1 tablespoon (15 ml) alcohol-free vanilla extract

1 tablespoon (7.5 g) lecithin

Pinch of sea salt (optional)

⅓ cup (80 ml) coconut oil, warmed to liquid

1. Place the strawberries, cashews, water, coconut meat, agave, vanilla, lecithin, and salt into a high-power blender and process until very smooth.
2. Add the coconut oil and blend again.
3. Chill the mixture and then process in an ice cream maker according to the manufacturer's instructions.
4. Place in the freezer to firm.

Maple-Pecan Ice Cream

Makes about 5 cups (750 g)
Soak time: 2 hours
Prep time: 25 minutes
Chill time: 2 hours

1 cup (120 g) cashews, soaked 2 hours

1¹⁄₃ cups (315 ml) water

²⁄₃ cup (53 g) young Thai coconut meat

²⁄₃ cup (230 g) maple syrup

1 tablespoon (15 ml) alcohol-free vanilla extract

1 tablespoon (7.5 g) lecithin powder

Pinch of sea salt (optional)

¼ cup (60 ml) coconut oil, warmed to liquid

1 cup (100 g) chopped pecans or Sweet & Spicy Candied Pecans (see page 155)

1. Place the cashews, water, coconut meat, maple syrup, vanilla, lecithin, and salt into a high-power blender and process until very smooth.
2. Add the coconut oil and blend again.
3. Chill the mixture and then process in an ice cream maker according to the manufacturer's instructions.
4. Fold in the pecans and place in the freezer to firm.

Dark Chocolate Brownie Chunk Ice Cream

Makes 5 cups (750 g)
Soak time: 2 hours
Prep time: 45 minutes
Chill time: 2 hours

BROWNIES

²⁄₃ cup (66 g) walnuts, soaked 6–8 hours and dehydrated

½ cup (72 g) Medjool dates

3 tablespoons (15 g) cacao powder

Pinch of sea salt (optional)

ICE CREAM

1 cup (120 g) cashews, soaked 2 hours

¾ cup (60 g) young Thai coconut meat

1 cup (235 ml) water

½ cup (170 g) agave nectar

¾ cup (60 g) cacao powder

1 tablespoon (7.5 g) lecithin powder

Pinch of sea salt (optional)

¼ cup (55 g) cacao butter, warmed to liquid

BROWNIES

1. In a food processor, grind the walnuts into a flour.
2. Add the dates, cacao powder, and sea salt and process again until it turns into a dough.
3. Use a rolling pin to flatten out the mixture about ¼ inch (6 mm) thick onto a nonstick surface and chill to firm.
4. Cut the mixture into little cubes.

ICE CREAM

1. Place the cashews, coconut meat, water, agave, cacao powder, lecithin, and salt into a high-power blender and process until very smooth.
2. Add the cacao butter and blend again.
3. Chill the mixture and then process in an ice cream maker according to the manufacturer's instructions.
4. Fold in the brownie bits and place in the freezer to firm.

Ice Box Chocolate Chip Cookies

Makes 12 to 14 cookies
Prep time: 30 minutes

If you enjoy frozen cookie dough, then you're going to love this simple recipe. Try making an ice cream sandwich using two cookies filled with Basic Vanilla Bean Ice Cream (see page 139).

1½ cups (180 g) cashews

⅔ cup (97 g) Medjool dates

3 tablespoons (48 g) almond butter

⅛ teaspoon sea salt (optional)

¼ cup (44 g) chocolate chips*

1. In a food processor, grind the cashews into a flour.
2. Add the dates, almond butter, and sea salt and process until it sticks together. Use a spatula to scrape down the sides as needed.
3. Transfer to a bowl and mix in the chocolate chips with a spatula or your hands. If you're not using tempered chocolate, add the chips after you roll out the dough, or else they will melt.
4. Roll the dough with a rolling pin on a nonstick sheet or parchment paper, making the dough about ⅜ inch (1 cm) thick (a).
5. Cut out with a cookie cutter and freeze (b). These are best served frozen.

The cookies will keep for 1 month in the freezer.

*Chop Basic Raw Chocolate (see page 147) into chips or use store-bought raw chocolate or chocolate chips.

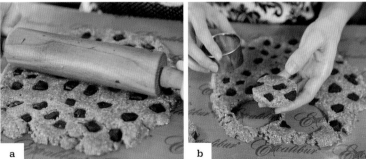

a

b

White Chocolate Cherry Cheesecake

Makes 12 servings
Soak time: 2 hours
Prep time: 45 minutes
Chill time: 2 hours

This classic cheesecake will make anyone want to go raw. The crunchy, salted texture of the crust, the creamy cake, and the sweet, tart cherries make this one of the superstar desserts in my collection.

CRUST

2¼ cups (225 g) walnuts, soaked 6–8 hours and dehydrated

⅓ cup (48 g) Medjool dates

¼ cup (30 g) palm sugar

¼ cup (20 g) cacao powder

¼ cup (44 g) cacao nibs

⅛ teaspoon sea salt

FILLING

3 cups (360 g) cashews, soaked 2 hours

1 cup (235 ml) Basic Nut Milk (see page 160)

¾ cup (255 g) agave nectar

¼ cup (60 ml) lemon juice

2 tablespoons (30 ml) vanilla extract

¼ cup (30 g) lecithin powder

¾ cup (164 g) cacao butter, warmed to liquid

TOPPING

2 cups (310 g) fresh or frozen cherries, pitted and thawed

CRUST

1. In a food processor, grind the walnuts into a flour (a).
2. Add the dates and palm sugar and process until incorporated.
3. Add the cacao powder, cacao nibs, and sea salt and process again until the mixture starts to stick together (b).
4. Reserve ¼ cup (60 g) of the crust for the topping.
5. Spread the mixture evenly into a 9-inch (23-cm) springform pan lined with parchment paper (c).
6. Starting in the center, press the mixture firmly and work your way out (d).
7. Make the crust as even as possible. Don't forget the edges (e & f).

FILLING

1. Place the cashews, nut milk, agave, lemon juice, and vanilla into a high-power blender and process until very smooth. Add the lecithin and cacao butter and blend again.
2. Pour the filling onto the crust (g).
3. Smooth using an offset spatula (h).

recipe continues...

4. Spread 1 cup (155 g) of the cherries over the top of the filling, staggering them evenly (i).

5. Use a toothpick to gently push the cherries into the filling (j). Alternatively, you can spread the cherries over the crust and pour the filling over them. I prefer to place them myself so I have an evenly polka-dotted cheesecake.

6. Spread the remaining cherries over the top in the empty areas. Gently press the cherries halfway down with your finger (k).

7. Sprinkle with the reserved crust mix (l).

8. Place the cheesecake in the freezer for 2 hours. Let thaw before serving.

Store in the freezer for 1 month or in the refrigerator for 3 days.

VARIATION: Substitute your favorite berries in place of cherries.

RECIPES FOR THE REVOLUTION 145

a

Basic Raw Chocolate

Makes 2 cups (275 ml)
Prep time: 15 minutes
Chill time: 30 minutes

This is the base to make your own personal chocolate bars and candies. It also makes a great dip for fresh strawberries and bananas.

1 cup cacao butter, shaved into small pieces (a)

1 cup (80 g) cacao powder

2-4 tablespoons (40 to 80 g) agave nectar, less if you prefer bittersweet chocolate

2 teaspoons alcohol-free vanilla extract

Pinch of sea salt (optional)

1. Melt cacao butter in a saucepan over very low heat (b & c). It should be warm, not hot and you should be able to touch the pan and the cacao butter without pain. Turn the heat on and off to regulate temperature and use a candy thermometer if necessary. Cacao butter melts between 95 and 98°F (35 and 37°C).

2. Stir in the cacao powder, agave nectar, vanilla extract, and salt and combine very well (d & e). Add in your favorite ingredients.

3. Pour your mixture into chocolate molds and let set in the freezer for at least 30 minutes before removing (f & g).

The chocolate will keep in refrigerator for at least 2 months.

NOTE: Chocolate can be tempermental. Be very careful not to get any water or steam into the mixture. The smallest amount can seize your chocolate and cause it to curdle. If that happens, melt additional cacao butter and stir in little by little until it becomes fluid again.

Fruit and Nut Bar

Makes 2¼ cups (529 ml) of batter
Prep time: 20 minutes
Chill time: 30 minutes

I was a big fan of the Cadbury's fruit and nut bars when I was a kid. This recipe tastes even better and is much better for you.

1 recipe Basic Raw Chocolate (see page 146), melted

2 tablespoons (18 g) chopped almonds or nut of your choice

1 tablespoon (8 g) dried blueberries

1 tablespoon (9 g) dried Zante currants

1 tablespoon (8 g) finely chopped dried cherries

Stir all the ingredients together in a mixing bowl and pour into candy bar molds. Let set in the freezer for at least 30 minutes before removing.

The bars will keep in the refrigerator for at least 2 months.

VARIATIONS: Try adding different flavors to your chocolate, such as cayenne pepper if you like a kick or mint extract for coolness. Essential oils such as lavender, orange, or rosemary can give your chocolate bars your own artisan touch. Just make sure your oils are pure and food-grade.

NUTRITION NOTE: Raw cacao is high in minerals, especially magnesium and iron, and according to David Wolfe's book, *Superfoods*, contains the highest concentration of antioxidants of any food in the world.

Superfood Chocolate Bar

Makes 2¼ cups (529 ml) of batter
Prep time: 20 minutes
Chill time: 30 minutes

This chocolate bar is chock-full of goodness, but it's only a guideline. Feel free to pick and choose your favorite superfoods and create your own personal chocolate bar. You don't have to use everything I've listed, because some items may be a little more difficult to find.

1 recipe Basic Raw Chocolate (see page 146), melted

2 tablespoons (11 g) hemp seeds

1 tablespoon (80 g) chopped walnuts

1 tablespoon (8 g) dried blueberries

1 tablespoon (80 g) goji berries

¼ teaspoon maca powder

Pinch of spirulina or blue-green algae

Stir all the ingredients together in a mixing bowl and pour into candy bar molds. Let set in the freezer for at least 30 minutes.

Chef's Tip: You can also use mini cupcake liners or an ice cube tray if you don't have candy molds.

Snacks

Instead of going for the processed snacks full of artificial ingredients, reach for some sweet, salty, crunchy goodness made at home with the best ingredients around. Double the recipes and store them in an airtight container in the refrigerator so you always have a healthy snack on hand.

Teriyaki Coconut Jerky

Prep time: 20 minutes
Marinating time: 8 hours
Drying time: 12 hours

If you have a hankerin' for something meaty, then you're in for a treat. These are super flavorful and chewy and much better for you than the popular meat jerkies that contain cancer-causing sodium nitrates.

MARINADE
¼ cup (60 ml) tamari
3 tablespoons (60 g) liquid honey or agave nectar
1 teaspoon toasted sesame oil
1 tablespoon (8 g) grated ginger
1 clove garlic, crushed

2 cups (160 g) young Thai coconut meat, cut into large pieces

1. Whisk all the marinade ingredients together in a medium-size bowl.
2. Add the coconut and marinate for 8 hours or overnight.
3. Shake off the excess marinade, place on a mesh dehydrator tray, and dry at 110°F (43°C) for 12 hours or until dry.
4. Cut into bite-size pieces and store in an airtight container in the refrigerator for up to 1 week.

Basic Flax Crackers

Makes 2 dozen crackers
Soak time: 1 hour
Prep time: 10 minutes
Drying time: 9 hours

Here is the perfect, crunchy cracker for your favorite dips and cheeses. Try adding seasonings such as caraway seeds, onion powder, garlic powder, Italian herbs, curry powder, or chili powder to create your own unique crackers.

2 cups (336 g) brown or golden flaxseeds

2½ cups (595 ml) water

2 tablespoons (30 ml) tamari

1. Soak the flaxseeds in the water for 1 hour or until the liquid is absorbed.
2. Add the tamari and mix well.
3. Divide the mixture between 2 dehydrator trays (about 2¼ cups [530 ml] each) lined with nonstick sheets (a).
4. Spread the mixture evenly over the entire tray using an offset spatula (b, c & d). Dry at 145°F (63°C) for 1 hour.
5. Use a bash and chop or spatula to score into desired-size pieces and dry at 110°F (43°C) for 6 hours (e).
6. Flip onto a mesh dehydrator tray and dry for an additional 2 hours or until dry and crispy (f, g, & h).

The crackers will keep for 1 month in an airtight container.

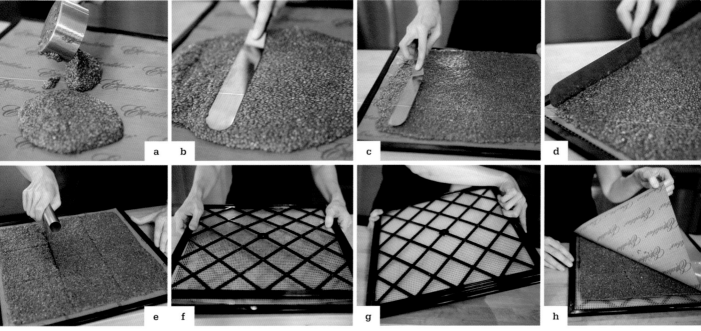

a   b   c   d

e   f   g   h

Sun-Dried Tomato and Herb Flax Crackers

Makes 2 dozen crackers
Soak time: 1 hour
Prep time: 15 minutes
Drying time: 9 hours

You don't have to use two different kinds of flaxseeds for these crackers. I just think they look prettier. These are great with Zucchini Hummus (see page 97) or Herbed Cashew Hemp Cheese (see page 100).

1 cup (168 g) golden flaxseeds

1 cup (168 g) brown flaxseeds

2½ cups (595 ml) water

6 tablespoons (42 g) sun-dried tomato powder*

¼ cup (40 g) finely minced onion

2 tablespoons (30 ml) tamari

2 tablespoons (30 ml) lemon juice

1 teaspoon Italian seasoning

2 cloves garlic, crushed or finely minced

1. Soak the flaxseeds in the water for 1 hour or until the liquid is absorbed. Add the tomato powder, onion, tamari, lemon juice, seasoning, and garlic and mix well.

2. Divide the mixture between 2 dehydrator trays (about 2¼ cups [530 ml] each) lined with nonstick sheets. Spread the mixture evenly over the entire tray using an offset spatula. Dry at 145°F (63°C) for 1 hour.

3. Score into desired-size pieces and dry at 110°F (43°C) for 6 hours.

4. Flip onto a mesh dehydrator tray and dry for an additional 2 hours or until dry and crispy.

The crackers will keep for 1 month in an airtight container.

*To make sun-dried tomato powder, process dried tomatoes in a food processor or blender until it becomes a fine powder.

NUTRITION NOTE: Flaxseeds are high in essential fatty acids omega-3 and -6. Grinding the seeds releases their full nutrient content, but I prefer the flavor and texture of whole seeds for my crackers. I just make sure to chew them well.

Spicy Hot Zucchini Chips

Makes 2 servings
Prep time: 10 minutes
Drying time: 8 to 10 hours

These light, crispy chips are so addictive!

2 medium-size zucchini (about 3 cups [339 g] when sliced)

3 tablespoons (45 ml) apple cider vinegar

2 tablespoons (30 ml) olive oil

2 teaspoons garlic powder

2 teaspoons onion powder

1 teaspoon Italian seasoning

½ teaspoon smoked paprika

½ teaspoon sea salt

¼ teaspoon cayenne pepper

1. Use a mandoline to slice the zucchini into ¹⁄₁₆-inch-thick (1.5 mm) chips and place in a medium-size bowl.

2. In a small bowl, combine the vinegar, oil, garlic powder, onion powder, Italian seasoning, paprika, salt, and cayenne (it will be pasty). Spread over the chips. Toss gently with your hands. *Hint:* Rub the Italian seasoning between your fingers to reactivate the oils.

3. Lay the chips on a mesh dehydrator sheet and dry at 110°F (46°C) for 8 to 10 hours or until crispy.

The chips will keep in an airtight container for 1 month. Return to the dehydrator if they get soft.

Cheesy Kale Crisps

Makes 4–6 servings
Soak time: 2 hours
Prep time: 10 minutes
Drying time: 6 to 7 hours

What better way to enjoy your greens than in this fun and crunchy, cheesy crisp.

2 bunches curly kale

1⅓ cups (160 g) cashews, soaked 2 hours

⅔ cup (160 ml) water

3 tablespoons (45 ml) lemon juice

2 tablespoons (32 g) chickpea miso or sweet or light miso paste

2 tablespoons (15 g) nutritional yeast

1 teaspoon paprika

1 teaspoon sea salt

1. Remove the kale from its stems and place the unshredded leaves in a large-size mixing bowl. I like to keep the pieces large.

2. Place the cashews, water, lemon juice, miso, nutritional yeast, paprika, and salt in a blender and process until smooth, scraping down the sides as needed. Add more water if needed to keep the blades moving, 1 tablespoon (15 ml) at a time. Less is better.

3. Pour the cheese mixture over the kale and use your hands to coat evenly.

4. Spread over 2 mesh dehydrator screens and dry at 110°F (46°C) for 6 to 7 hours or until crisp.

The crisps will keep in an airtight container for 1 month. Return to the dehydrator if they get soft.

Crispy Seasoned Onion Rings

Makes 4 servings
Soak time: 1 to 2 hours
Prep time: 20 minutes
Drying time: 8 hours

You can skip soaking the onions if you don't mind stronger-flavored onion rings, or use Vidalia onions when they're in season; these are a mild, sweet onion. Serve these with BBQ Veggie Burgers (see page 122) or just enjoy them on their own as a snack.

1 large or 2 medium-size sweet white or yellow onions

3 tablespoons (54 g) plus 1½ teaspoons sea salt

1 tablespoon (15 ml) lemon juice

½ cup (120 ml) Basic Nut Milk (see page 160)

1½ cups (168 g) ground golden flaxseeds

1½ tablespoons (13 g) garlic powder

¼ teaspoon cayenne pepper

¼ teaspoon freshly ground black pepper

1. Use a mandoline or a chef's knife to slice the onion into ¼-inch-thick (6 mm) rings and place in a medium-size bowl with the 3 tablespoons (54 g) sea salt and lemon juice, and cover with ice cold water. Allow to sit for 1 to 2 hours to mellow out the pungency. Rinse and drain when ready. Remove the onion skins if needed.

2. Pour the nut milk into a small bowl and set aside.

3. Combine the flaxseeds, garlic powder, remaining 1½ teaspoons sea salt, cayenne, and black pepper in a bowl. Place one-fourth of the mixture on a plate.

4. Dip each onion ring into the nut milk, shake off the excess moisture, and then dredge in the flaxseed mixture (a).

5. Place on a mesh dehydrator tray (b).

6. When your flax mixture becomes too moist to stick to the onion rings, discard it and add another one-fourth of the mixture. Continue until it becomes too moist again. Repeat until all the rings are coated.

7. Dry at 110°F (43°C) for 8 hours or until crispy.

The onion rings will keep in the refrigerator for 1 week.

a

b

Protein Crunch Mix

Makes 3 cups (300 g)
Soak time: 4 to 6 hours
Prep time: 10 minutes
Drying time: 8 hours

This high-protein mix (about 11 grams per ¼ cup [25 g]) makes a great addition to salads when you want a little crunch, or just eat it as a snack. I keep a small container of it in my car for when I'm on the go.

1½ cups (246 g) hulled buckwheat groats, soaked 1 hour

¾ cup (109 g) sunflower seeds, soaked 4–6 hours

¾ cup (105 g) pumpkin seeds, soaked 4–6 hours

5 tablespoons (75 ml) tamari

2 teaspoons onion powder

1 teaspoon garlic powder

1. Rinse and drain the buckwheat groats very well along with the sunflower and pumpkin seeds.

2. In a medium-size bowl, combine all the ingredients and spread over 2 dehydrator trays lined with nonstick sheets. Dry at 110°F (43°C) for 8 hours or until completely dry.

The mix will keep for 1 month in an airtight container.

Sweet & Spicy Candied Pecans

Makes 3 cups (300 g)
Prep time: 15 minutes
Drying time: 2 to 3 hours

This is a fun treat to put on your salad, in Maple Pecan Ice Cream (see page 140), or just to snack on. If you want it sweet without the spice, just omit the cayenne and black pepper.

¾ cup (90 g) finely ground palm sugar

¼ cup (80 g) maple syrup

1 teaspoon (2 g) cinnamon

¾ teaspoon (5 g) sea salt

¼ teaspoon cayenne pepper

¼ teaspoon freshly ground black pepper

3 cups (300 g) whole pecan halves, soaked 2–4 hours and dehydrated

1. Combine the palm sugar, maple syrup, cinnamon, sea salt, cayenne, and black pepper in a bowl until it becomes a thick paste.

2. Add the pecans and mix until all pieces are coated.

3. Spread the pecans over a mesh dehydrator tray, flat side down, and dry at 110°F (43°C) for 2 to 3 hours or until completely dry.

Store in an airtight container for up to 2 weeks.

Trail Mix Energy Bars

Makes 12 servings
Soak time: 30 minutes
Prep time: 20 minutes
Drying time: 12 hours

Kids love these sticky, chunky bars. They're great for athletes or for when you're on the go.

⅔ cup (87 g) dried apricots, soaked 30 minutes

¾ cup (109 g) Medjool dates

2 tablespoons (40 g) thick raw honey

1 tablespoon (15 ml) vanilla extract

1¼ cups (181 g) almonds, soaked 8–12 hours and dehydrated

¾ cup (60 g) shredded coconut

¾ cup (60 g) rolled oats

¾ cup (90 g) dried cranberries

⅓ cup (47 g) pumpkin seeds, soaked 4–6 hours and dehydrated

¼ teaspoon sea salt

1. Place the apricots, dates, honey, and vanilla in a food processor and blend until it becomes a paste. Use a spatula to scrape down the sides as needed.

2. Add the almonds, coconut, oats, cranberries, pumpkin seeds, and salt and pulse several times until incorporated. Depending on the size of your food processor, you might have to do this in 2 batches. Don't overprocess. It's nice to see large pieces of fruit and nuts.

3. Press the mixture firmly into an 8 x 8-inch (20 x 20-cm) baking pan lined with parchment paper.

4. Put the pan in the dehydrator and dry at 110°F (43°C) for 6 hours.

5. Flip onto a mesh dehydrator tray and dry for another 6 hours.

6. Cut into desired-size pieces.

Stored in an airtight container in the refrigerator, the energy bars will keep for 2 weeks.

Beverages

Stay hydrated and radiant with these nutrient and antioxidant rich beverages.

Ruby Red Ginger and Honey Sun Tea

Makes 4 cups (950 ml)

This lovely, crimson tea is really a health tonic in disguise. Hibiscus flower has a tart and fruity flavor and is superhigh in vitamin C. Used for centuries in herbal medicine, it has recently been shown in studies to lower high blood pressure and high cholesterol. Ginger is a powerful anti-inflammatory and is beneficial for circulation, arthritis, nausea, and lessening cold and flu symptoms, and may prevent migraines if taken early. Raw honey has antifungal, antibacterial, and antimicrobial properties as well as cancer-preventing, antitumor properties. Pretty impressive for a glass of sun tea. Now drink up!

4 cups (950 ml) water
3 tablespoons (9 g) dried crushed hibiscus flowers
4 teaspoons ginger juice*
⅓ cup (115 g) honey
Lime wedge for garnish

1. Place the water and hibiscus leaves in a glass jar and close with a lid.
2. Allow to sit in the sunshine for 6 hours.
3. Pour the tea through a strainer into a pitcher and add the ginger juice and honey.
4. Chill before serving, then garnish with a lime wedge.

The tea will keep for 3 days in the refrigerator.

*To make ginger juice, run ginger root through a juicer or grate ginger and squeeze it through a nut milk bag.

Red Wine Sangria

Makes 6 to 8 servings
Prep time: 20 minutes
Chill time: 2 hours

Traditional Spanish sangria is usually made with a little bit of this and a little bit of that, so you don't need to adhere strictly to this recipe. I use whatever fruits are in season to make mine. In the summer I use peaches and different berries, and in the fall I like to use apples and pears.

1 bottle (750 ml) dry red wine (Merlot, Cabernet, or Shiraz)

Juice of 2 oranges

Juice of 1 lime

Juice of 1 lemon

½ cup (170 g) agave nectar

2 apples, cored and chopped

1 lime, thinly sliced for garnish

1 lemon, thinly sliced for garnish

1 orange, thinly sliced for garnish

4 cups (950 ml) sparkling mineral water (Perrier or San Pellegrino are good)

1. In a large pitcher, mix the red wine, orange juice, lime juice, lemon juice, agave nectar, and apples and chill in the refrigerator for 2 hours.

2. Before serving, add the lime, lemon, and orange slices and sparkling water to the pitcher. Stir and serve over ice.

NUTRITION TIP: Choose an organic red wine with no added sulfites to make your sangria. Your head will thank you in the morning … unless you drink too much of it.

Basic Nut Milk

Makes 4 servings
Soak time: 2 to 12 hours
Prep time: 5 minutes

Once you start making your own fresh nut milk, you'll never want to go back to the boxed stuff again.

BASIC NUT MILK

1 cup (145 g) nuts, soaked*

4 cups (950 ml) water

SWEETENED VANILLA NUT MILK

1 cup (145 g) nuts, soaked*

4 cups (950 ml) water

2 or 3 Medjool dates, 2 table-spoons (40 g) agave nectar or honey, or dash of stevia

½ scraped vanilla bean or 1 tablespoon vanilla extract

Pinch of sea salt (optional)

BASIC NUT MILK

1. Process the nuts and water in a blender (a), then strain the pulp through a nut milk bag (b).

SWEETENED VANILLA NUT MILK

1. Process the nuts and water in a blender (a), then strain the pulp through a nut milk bag (b).
2. Rinse the blender container and pour the nut milk back in with the dates, scraped vanilla bean, and sea salt and blend again.

Store in the refrigerator for up to 3 days. Shake before using.

*Soaking times will depend on which nuts you use. You can also use seeds or a combination of both. My personal favorites are Brazil nut milk and almond milk. See the Soak Times chart on pages 46–47 to plan your recipe preparation.

NOTE: You can make a nondairy creamer by using a 1:2 ratio of nuts to water.

Chef's Tip: The leftover nut pulp can be dehydrated and then ground into a fine flour to use for desserts. Store the flour in an airtight container in the refrigerator. This flour will last for several months.

a

b

Coconut Chai Cooler

Makes 2 servings
Prep time: 15 minutes

2 cups (475 ml) young Thai coconut water

²/₃ cup (60 g) young Thai coconut meat

1 tablespoon (20 g) agave nectar

2 teaspoons chai spice mix

1 teaspoon lecithin powder

1 cup (145 g) ice cubes

Cinnamon for garnish

1. Place all the ingredients in a high-power blender and process until smooth. Adjust to taste if you like it sweeter or spicier.
2. Garnish with cinnamon before serving.

Blueberry Lemonade

Makes 3 or 4 servings
Prep time: 15 minutes

The ultimate summer drink. This works with strawberries as well, though I like to mash the strawberries with a fork instead of puréeing them.

1¼ cups (180 g) blueberries, fresh or frozen, thawed

3 cups (710 ml) water

1 cup (145 g) ice cubes

½ cup (120 ml) lemon juice

¼ cup (85 g) agave nectar

1. Purée 1 cup (145 g) of the blueberries in a food processor.
2. Transfer to a pitcher, add the water, ice, lemon juice, agave, and remaining ¼ cup (35 g) blueberries and stir.

The lemonade will keep for 1 day in the refrigerator.

Living and Fermented Foods

Fermented foods repopulate the gut with beneficial bacteria. Many people have digestive problems that stem from an overabundance of bad bacteria in the intestines, such as candida, a yeast that forms from a high-sugar diet. By adding good bacteria we can keep the bad bacteria in check, boost our immune system, improve digestion, and bring our bodies back into balance. People who eat fermented foods report having better skin, more energy, and fewer sugar cravings.

Coconut Kefir

Makes 8 to 16 servings
Prep time: 15 minutes
Fermentation time: 36 to 48 hours

4 cups (950 ml) fresh young Thai coconut water (4 or 5 coconuts)

Kefir starter (I recommend Body Ecology)

1 quart (946-ml) jar with lid

1. Warm the coconut water in a saucepan to about 92° to 98°F (33 to 37°C). Dissolve 1 packet (5 grams) of kefir starter in the coconut water (a).

2. Pour the coconut water into a 1-quart (946-ml) glass jar and close tightly (b). Allow to ferment for 36 to 48 hours at room temperature (72° to 75°F [22° to 24°C]). Fermented coconut water will become milky white and will form bubbles at the top. The taste should be slightly bubbly, tart, and tangy.

Drink ¼ to ½ cup (60 to 120 ml) every morning, with meals, and before bed.

Store in the refrigerator and consume within 1 week.

You can start another batch of kefir by taking 6 tablespoons (90 ml) of fermented coconut kefir and adding it to fresh coconut water and repeating the fermentation process. It's best to make the transfer within 3 days. This can be done 7 times before you need to start with new kefir culture starter.

Coconut Yogurt

Makes 8 to 12 servings
Prep time: 15 minutes
Fermentation time: 7 to 10 hours

After you make Coconut Kefir (see page 162) you can use the remaining coconut meat to make this creamy yogurt. Use it the same way you would use plain yogurt, in smoothies, with fruit and honey, or with cinnamon and other flavorings, but be careful—this yogurt is high in fat, so watch your portions.

3 to 4 cups (240 to 320 g) young Thai coconut meat

Filtered water or coconut water

Kefir starter

1 quart (946-ml) jar with lid

a

1. Place the coconut meat in a high-power blender and add just enough filtered water to create a creamy pudding (a).
2. Transfer to a mixing bowl and stir in ½ packet (2.5 grams) of kefir starter and pour into the jar. You may use a smaller jar, but be sure to allow a few inches at the top for the yogurt to expand.
3. Let ferment for 7 to 10 hours at room temperature (72° to 75°F [22° to 24°C]).

Keep sealed in the refrigerator for up to 3 days.

Chef's Tip: The most important thing to remember when making fermented foods and beverages is to use sterile jars, lids, crocks, bowls, and utensils. Running them through the dishwasher or pouring boiling water on them will help prevent bad bacteria from ruining the batch.

SERVING SUGGESTION:
MANGO LASSI

Makes 2 servings
Prep time: 10 minutes

2 cups (350 g) frozen mango

½ cup (115 g) Coconut Yogurt

½ cup (120 ml) water

1 to 2 tablespoons (20 to 40 g) agave, or sweeten with honey or stevia

Pinch of cardamom (optional)

Blend all ingredients and serve cold.

Traditional Fermented Sauerkraut

Prep time: 1 hour
Fermentation time: 1 to 4 weeks

Being Eastern European, I grew up on sauerkraut and have always loved its sharp, tangy flavor. Unfortunately, most of the sauerkraut found in the supermarkets is not fermented but instead pickled in vinegar and pasteurized, and therefore nutritionally null. Here's the old-time, traditional method for you to make it at home—it tastes amazing and is also a powerful digestive aid and immune system booster.

Cabbage

Ceramic crock or wide-mouth jar

Sea salt

German-made crocks are terrific for making foolproof sauerkraut. The *Gartopf* ("fermentation pot") is a treat to own but can be a little pricey, so I am going to show you the inexpensive route that uses items you probably have around your house.

The amount of cabbage you will need depends upon the size of the container you will be using. One head of cabbage for each quart (L) usually works.

I have a 1-gallon (4 L) jar, so I will be using 3 heads of cabbage, leaving a bit of room at the top to add my weight.

1 head of cabbage = 1 quart (946 ml)
2 teaspoons (12 g) of salt per head of cabbage

1. Remove a few of the outer leaves and set aside (a). Discard any that have mold on them.
2. Quarter each head of cabbage and remove the core (b). Finely shred the cabbage using a mandoline, a knife, or the shredding plate on a food processor (c).
3. Transfer to a large bowl and add salt (d). Massage the cabbage until water begins to release (e). Allow to sit for 10 minutes or more and then massage again until it gets very watery. Repeat a few times until the cabbage is very juicy (f).

a

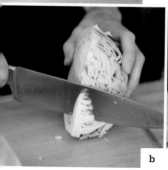

b

c

d

e

4. Transfer the cabbage to a container and pack very firmly so that the cabbage is fully submerged in water (g & h). If you don't have enough water, dissolve 2 teaspoons (12 g) of salt per 1 cup (235 ml) of water and add to the container. Place your reserved leaves over the cabbage, letting the leaves extend partially up the sides (i).

5. Put a weight on the leaves, such as a jar filled with water or a clean, sterilized rock, and make sure the cabbage is fully submerged (j). Cover with a clean towel and place in the corner of your kitchen. Ferment at room temperature for a few days, up to 4 weeks, depending on how tart you like it and how warm the environment is. Do not store below 65°F (18°C) or it will not ferment.

6. For the first 2 days, gently press on the weight several times a day, or when you remember, to keep the sauerkraut packed firmly. You will notice within the first day or two fermentation bubbles forming in the brine.

7. It is normal for slime to occasionally form on the surface. Just scrape off as much as you can. As long as the sauerkraut is submerged in the brine, it will not be affected.

8. Taste your sauerkraut every few days for flavor. Once it is to your liking, remove the top leaves and transfer the mixture with the salt brine into glass jars and store in the refrigerator. It can last several weeks, though it goes quick around my house.

You can add other vegetables to your kraut before you ferment, such as shredded carrots, beets, turnips, onions, or even apples, as well as seasonings such as garlic, ginger, dill, bay leaves, or caraway seeds.

f g h i j

RECIPES FOR THE REVOLUTION 165

Kimchi

Makes 2 quarts (2 L)
Prep time: 1 to 1 ½ hours
Fermentation time: 1 to 2 weeks

Kimchi is a hot and spicy, traditional Korean dish made with napa cabbage and various spices. This recipe is courtesy of Matt Samuelson, former head chef and instructor at Living Light. Make this as you would the Traditional Fermented Sauerkraut (see page 164). Ingredients are different, but the process is still the same.

2 heads napa (Chinese) cabbage

3 large carrots, shredded

1 yellow onion, cut into ⅛-inch-thick (3 mm) half-moons

1 medium-size daikon radish, cut into ⅛-inch-thick (3 mm) half-moons

5 cloves garlic, coarsely chopped

2 inches (5 cm) fresh ginger, peeled and finely grated or microplaned

1 tablespoon (19 g) sea salt

2 teaspoons red pepper flakes

3-quart or 1-gallon (3 or 4 L) jar

Smaller jar filled with water or sanitized stone

1. Remove a few outer napa cabbage leaves and set aside.

2. Use a knife to slice the leafy parts of the cabbage into ¾-inch (2-cm) ribbons and set aside.

3. With a mandoline or a knife, shred the thick, white parts into ⅜-inch (1-cm) ribbons. Place in a bowl. Add the carrots, onion, daikon, garlic, and ginger.

4. Massage the salt into the mixture for a few minutes, allow to rest for 10 minutes, and then massage again. Repeat until the mixture is very juicy.

5. Add the reserved cabbage ribbons and red pepper flakes and mix well. Don't massage, or the leaves will become too mushy and your hands will burn!

6. Pack the mixture firmly into the larger jar and top with the reserved outer cabbage leaves. Place the smaller jar on top and press down. If the water level is not well above the cabbage leaves, mix 1 teaspoon (6 g) of sea salt with 1 cup (235 ml) of water and add to the jar until the water level is about 1 inch (2.5 cm) above and no leaves are sticking out of the salt brine.

7. Cover with a towel and keep at room temperature for 1–2 weeks. For the first couple days press the weight jar regularly to keep the mixture packed. If you prefer it tangy, ferment for 2 weeks.

8. If a slime appears on the surface, use a spoon to remove it. This is normal. Your kimchi will be unaffected if it is submerged in the brine.

9. When ready, remove the top leaves and transfer the mixture with the salt brine into glass jars and store in the refrigerator.

Rejuvelac

Makes 4 cups
Soak time: 8 to 12 hours
Sprouting time: 2 days
Fermentation time: 36 to 48 hours

Rejuvelac is a fermented beverage made with the soak water of wheat berries and other grains. It was originally made famous by raw food health pioneer Ann Wigmore, who recommended it to her patients as a digestive tonic. I mainly use it as a starter for nut and seed cheese to give it a nice tart, sharp flavor. You can substitute or combine with other grains, such as kamut or spelt, though rye is my favorite.

2 cups (368 g) rye or soft wheat berries

Purified water

2-quart (2-L) glass jar with mesh sprouting lid

1. Place the grains in a 2-quart (2-L) glass jar filled with at least 4 cups (950 ml) of water for 8 to 12 hours. Drain and rinse and store at a 45-degree angle so that air can still circulate in the jar.

2. Sprout for 2 days, rinsing at least twice a day. Rinse multiple times until the water is clear. Once you see the tails emerge out of the seeds, rinse two to three times, until the water runs clear, and then fill the jar with purified water. Cover the mouth of the jar with cheesecloth and a rubber band.

3. Keep at room temperature (72° to 75°F [22° to 24°C]) in a shady spot and allow to ferment for 36 to 48 hours or until you achieve the desired tartness. Pour the liquid into a container and store in the refrigerator. It should appear slightly yellow and cloudy and have a lemony, tart flavor. It will become very sour once it is past its prime.

You can make an additional batch by soaking the sprouted seeds in water for another 24 hours. Pour off the liquid into a container and give the seeds to the birds or the compost bin.

Store in an airtight container in the refrigerator for 2 or 3 days.

Quick and Easy Extras

Bring your raw food creations together with these quick and easy extras.

BBQ Sauce

Makes 1 cup (250 g)
Soak time: 1–2 hours
Prep time: 15 minutes

Use this for the BBQ Veggie Burgers (see page 122) or Crispy Seasoned Onion Rings (see page 153), or slather it over vegetable kebabs made with zucchini, bell peppers, and pineapples and dehydrate until soft and tender. So good!

½ cup (23 g) sun-dried tomatoes, soaked 1–2 hours, soak water reserved

2 tablespoons (30 ml) soak water, or more as needed

2 tablespoons (30 ml) olive oil

2 tablespoons (30 ml) tamari

2 tablespoons (20 g) diced white or yellow onion

1 tablespoon (20 g) honey or agave nectar

2 teaspoons apple cider vinegar

1 small clove garlic

1 teaspoon dried mustard

½ teaspoon black pepper

¼ teaspoon chipotle powder

¼ teaspoon sea salt

1. In a blender, process all the ingredients until smooth.
2. Adjust the seasonings for more sweet, salt, or spice.
3. If too thick, add more soak water, 1 tablespoon (15 ml) at a time, until you reach the desired consistency.

The sauce will keep for 1 week in the refrigerator.

Pico de Gallo

Makes 2½ cups (650 g)
Prep time: 15 minutes

2 cups (360 g) seeded and diced tomatoes

½ cup (80 g) diced yellow onion

¼ cup (4 g) finely chopped cilantro

1 serrano or jalapeño pepper, seeded and finely minced

2 tablespoons (30 g) lemon juice

1 clove garlic, crushed

½ teaspoon sea salt

Combine all the ingredients in a bowl and allow the flavors to mingle for at least 1 hour.

The pico de gallo will keep for 2 or 3 days in the refrigerator.

Parmesan Cheese

Makes ¾ cup (75 g)
Soak time: 2 hours
Prep time: 10 minutes
Drying time: 6 to 8 hours

Great on pizza or any of the Italian dishes.

½ cup (70 g) macadamia nuts, soaked 2 hours

¼ cup (35 g) pine nuts, soaked 2 hours

2 teaspoons lemon juice

2 teaspoons nutritional yeast

½ teaspoon sea salt

2 tablespoons (30 ml) water

1. Combine the nuts, lemon juice, nutritional yeast, and salt in a food processor, scraping down the sides, until well mixed. Add the water while processing to make it fluffy.

2. Spread the cheese thinly on a nonstick dehydrator sheet and dry at 110°F (43°C) for 6 to 8 hours. Process the cheese in a spice grinder for a few seconds to make it crumbly. Do not overprocess or it will become sticky.

The Parmesan Cheese will keep for 1 week in an airtight container in the refrigerator.

Sour Cream

Makes 1 cup (230 g)
Soak time: 2 hours
Prep time: 5 minutes

1 cup (120 g) cashews, soaked 2 hours

½ cup (120 ml) water, or more as needed

2 tablespoons (30 ml) lemon juice

¼ teaspoon sea salt

Place all the ingredients in a blender and process until smooth. Add more water if needed.

The sour cream will keep for 5 days in the refrigerator.

Quick and Easy Bites

SAVORY

Here are a few recipes that don't require more than a kitchen knife and just a few minutes of your time.

Romaine Wraps

Makes 1–2 servings
Prep time: 10 minutes

2 large romaine leaves

1 avocado, sliced

1 tomato, diced

1 tablespoon (9 g) pumpkin seeds

½ cup (25 g) sprouts

1 lime wedge

Dash of sea salt

Garlic Tahini Dressing (optional; see page 85)

1. Fill the romaine leaves with avocado, tomato, pumpkin seeds, and sprouts.
2. Squeeze the lime and sprinkle a dash of salt over the filling or drizzle with tahini dressing.

Jicama Fries

Makes 1–2 servings
Prep time: 10 minutes

1 small jicama, peeled

½ lime, cut into wedges

Dash of chili powder

Sea salt to taste

Slice the jicama into "fries." Spread over a plate, squeeze the lime wedges over all, and add a dash of chili powder and sea salt.

Guacamole Mushroom Caps

Makes 1–2 servings
Prep time: 10 minutes

1 cup (70 g) whole mushroom caps, cleaned

⅓ cup (75 g) Chunky Curried Guacamole (see page 102) or traditional guacamole

Remove the stems from the mushroom caps and fill with the guacamole.

Seaweed Salad

Makes 1–2 servings
Prep time: 15 minutes

¾ cup (60 g) arame seaweed, soaked 5 minutes

1 carrot

1 cucumber

2 tablespoons (30 ml) tamari

1 tablespoon (15 ml) brown rice vinegar

1 teaspoon agave nectar

Dash of red pepper flakes

Dash of black sesame seeds

1. While the arame is soaking, use a hand julienne peeler to shred the carrot and cucumber into strips. Rinse and drain the arame and toss with the vegetables.
2. Combine the tamari, vinegar, agave nectar, red pepper flakes, and sesame seeds in a small bowl and pour over the vegetables.

Cabbage Cup

Makes 1–2 servings
Prep time: 10 minutes

½ Roma tomato, chopped

¼ avocado, diced

3 baby portobello mushrooms, chopped

1 tablespoon (10 g) diced white onion

1 tablespoon (15 ml) tamari

1 red cabbage leaf

½ cup (25 g) alfalfa or other sprouts

Combine the tomato, avocado, mushrooms, onion, and tamari in a bowl. Fill the cabbage leaf with the mixture. Top with the sprouts.

Heirloom Tomato Carpaccio

Makes 1–2 servings
Prep time: 10 minutes

1 large heirloom or beefsteak tomato, thinly sliced

1 tablespoon (15 ml) olive oil

1 tablespoon (15 ml) balsamic vinegar

Sea salt and pepper to taste

1 tablespoon (2.5 g) chopped basil

1. Lay the tomato slices on a large plate and drizzle with olive oil and balsamic vinegar. Season with salt and pepper.
2. Garnish with the chopped basil.

Quick and Easy Bites

These sweet treats will curb your hunger and fuel you with raw energy any time of day.

Muesli Bowl

Makes 2 servings
Prep time: 10 minutes

¼ cup (20 g) rolled oats

½ apple, diced

½ banana, sliced

2 tablespoons (18 g) coarsely chopped almonds

2 tablespoons (18 g) raisins

1 tablespoon (9 g) sunflower seeds

1 tablespoon (5 g) shredded coconut

Dash of cinnamon

Basic or sweetened vanilla Nut Milk (see page 160)

Sweetener to taste (optional)

Combine all the ingredients in a bowl

Chocolate Ganache

Makes 2 servings
Prep time: 10 minutes
Chill time: 15 minutes

¼ cup (20 g) cacao powder

3 tablespoons (60 g) maple syrup

2 tablespoons (30 ml) coconut oil, warmed to liquid

Mix all the ingredients by hand or in a blender for a smoother texture. Pour into a small custard cup and chill in the freezer for 15 minutes or until firm.

Ants on a Log

Makes 1–2 servings
Prep time: 5 minutes

This is a good recipe for little kids and big (adult) kids alike.

1 large banana

1 to 2 tablespoons (16 to 32 g) almond butter

Dash of cinnamon

1 tablespoon (9 g) raisins

Smother the banana with the almond butter. Top with the cinnamon and raisins.

Honey-Almond Macaroons

Makes 2 servings
Prep time: 5 minutes
Chill time: 15 minutes

½ cup (40 g) shredded coconut

2 tablespoons (32 g) almond butter

1 tablespoon (20 g) thick raw honey

1 teaspoon vanilla extract

⅛ teaspoon sea salt

Combine all the ingredients in a bowl. Scoop heaping tablespoons of the mixture and form into balls. Chill in the freezer for 15 minutes or until firm.

Stuffed Date Rolls

Makes 2 servings
Prep time: 5 minutes

These rolls are tastier than any store-bought candy. You can use pecans and almonds as well.

4 Medjool dates

2 to 3 tablespoons (16 to 24 g) walnut halves or pieces

Remove the pits from the dates and stuff with walnut pieces. Use fresh dates if you can find them.

Chapter 4 # Successfully Raw

Raw food isn't just a diet; it's a lifestyle. Eating the best stuff on earth affects the way we look and feel and the way we see the world. It shouldn't be something we do for a little while and then move on to the next diet trend. We need to eat real foods every day and nourish ourselves if we want to live healthy lives.

How Much Raw Is Right for You?

There are myriad raw food opinions and well-meaning advice out there, but only you can determine how much raw food is right for you. Listen to your body and see how you feel. Longtime raw foodists are in tune with what their bodies need, and they develop a sense of which foods they should be eating when. Take note of how you feel after eating certain foods and see what works best for you.

If you live in a temperate area, going 100 percent raw can be difficult. During the winter months, fewer fresh, local fruits and vegetables are available, and our bodies tend to want foods that are warming. Many raw foodists who live in cold climates incorporate more cooked foods such as soups, cooked grains, root vegetables, and hard squash in the winter and eat more raw in the warmer months.

✸

I first discovered raw food at the weight of 400 pounds, a very scary time in my life. I switched overnight to a 100 percent raw lifestyle, and four years later I haven't been off since. Since that day I have lost more than 215 pounds and really created a new life for myself. Not only am I healthier, but I also left my job to pursue my passion of helping others and sharing what is possible once you take steps to love and accept yourself.

—*Philip McCluskey, author and motivational speaker, www.lovingraw.com*

MAKING THE TRANSITION

Unless you're a real go-getter, I don't recommend starting a 100 percent raw diet overnight. Be prepared mentally before you dive in to this lifestyle commitment, and have a game plan. My suggestions for transitioning into raw foods are:

Assess your life and set realistic goals. Your schedule may not allow you the time to prepare all your own raw food every day. Maybe pick one or two meals a day that you know you can manage, such as a smoothie for breakfast or a salad for lunch. Once you reach these small goals, start to set bigger goals, such as going one weekend or one week entirely raw.

✳ There is also a chance that a 100 percent raw diet isn't right for you. People with diabetes, irritable bowel syndrome, colitis, or other digestive disorders should consult a holistic physician before making any drastic changes to their diets.

Start slowly and have fun. A raw food journey can be really exciting or really overwhelming. If you're anxious and miserable about what you can and can't eat, you're not going to stick with it too long. Take your time, try new things, and have fun with it.

* Buy recipe books, visit raw food blogs, take raw food prep classes, attend raw food potlucks, and seek the fellowship of other raw foodists. Find a friend who wants to make the journey with you.

Once you set your goal, commit to it and be consistent. If you're going to quit coffee, quit coffee. If you want to quit dairy, quit dairy. I was a coffee and cheese addict before I went raw. If I'd kept giving in every time I had a craving, I would still be addicted to them. Today they have no allure to me. You can break any food addiction in time, but I recommend doing it one at a time.

What you don't eat may be more important than what you do eat. You may have added some fresh fruit and vegetables to your daily diet, but if you're still eating foods that are heavy or processed, you may not feel the benefits. Add raw foods to your diet but also let go of foods that slow you down or keep you from reaching your health goals.

·· ✸ ··

Raw food is a great tool to help you feel great, have more energy, and allow the body to heal naturally, but remember it's only a tool. Many people get caught up trying to maintain 100 percent raw and fail because they don't have the true goal in sight. The real focus should be on getting the best health for you, using all the health tools out there—a combination of eating, stress management, exercise, sleep, and relationship and job satisfaction. No one really wants a plaque on the wall, signed by all the raw food experts, that says they certifiably eat 100 percent. That doesn't mean anything (except to their ego). What does mean something is finding the right balance between the items I listed above and feeling absolutely amazing all the time. That's true optimal health.

—*Kevin Gianni, health advocate, cohost of* The Renegade Health Show,
author of High Raw, *www.renegadehealth.com*

···

Finding Balance

If I were to draw my own personal raw food pyramid, vegetables, green leafy vegetables, and sprouts would be the base. Fruits and grains (including sprouted buckwheat, kamut, quinoa, and oats) would be the second tier, and the very top would be fats such as avocados, nuts, and seeds. Though I've included some decadent recipes in here, please don't eat brownies and ice cream all day long and declare that you are raw. Focus on the greens, veggies, and fruits first, and then splurge on the other stuff when you need to.

What I Eat

On most days I eat a very simple diet. So simple that if I made a recipe book of what I normally eat on a daily basis, you probably would not have purchased this book or even wanted to try following a raw food diet. My typical day is:

* Green juice a couple of hours after I get up
* Small serving of seasonal fruit for breakfast
* Green smoothie with superfoods for lunch
* Hummus and flax crackers for snack
* Mixed green salad for dinner with sprouts, herbs, dulse strips, avocado, lemon juice, and a pinch of salt, or just soup if I'm not that hungry.

Mind you, I've been raw for four years. My appetite and diet naturally evolved into eating this style of menu. When I first went raw I needed familiar foods that reminded me of the cooked foods I used to eat. I also wanted that feeling of fullness that cooked food gave me, but surprisingly, within a few weeks of being 100 percent raw, I started to lose those cravings and wanted to eat simpler. It wasn't something I even thought about. My body was craving less fat, less salt, less concentrated sugar. My taste buds changed. I didn't need a ton of seasoning, and I started to appreciate the natural flavor of naked food. Almost every raw foodist experiences this phenomenon, and it's actually really liberating. I could spend less time in the kitchen because I was satisfied with a bowl of grapes for breakfast and romaine leaves with tomatoes, onions, sprouts, and tahini dressing for dinner. I still love gourmet raw foods, but I don't need them every day for each meal. Every couple of days works fine for me.

Raw Food Dogma

Some extreme raw foodists look at all cooked food as taboo. Eating cooked food is not a sin and it's not "cheating"; it's just a choice. There are no raw police looking over your shoulder. I choose to eat food that is as nutritious as possible, but sometimes I like to eat cooked food, especially when it's cold or when I travel and raw food options are few. In the end, food is a blessing. Whatever you choose to eat, eat in a positive state of mind, with thankfulness and never out of guilt or shame.

Easy Raw Tips and Tricks

Being prepared with your own food at mealtimes (or even between meals) is the best way to stick to a healthy diet and prevent reaching for processed convenience foods. Keep a few staples around so that you can throw together a quick meal or calm an impending snack attack.

* **Once a week make:**
  * One or two salad dressings that will last all week. Garlic Tahini and Creamy Dill (see page 85 for both) store well.
  * Nut milk for smoothies or granola cereal (see page 160)
  * One batch of Zucchini Hummus (see page 97)
  * A couple of snacks, such as Cheesy Kale Crisps or Spicy Hot Zucchini Chips (see page 152 for both)

* **Once a month make:**
  * A double batch of flax crackers (see page 150)
  * One batch of Maple Pecan Granola (see page 64)
  * One or two batches of Basic Raw Chocolate (see page 146)

* **Always keep on hand plenty of fresh fruit and vegetables to snack on, including:**
  * Collard greens to make a quick veggie wrap
  * Ripe avocados to whip up some guacamole
  * Frozen bananas for an easy, creamy smoothie
  * Nut butters to spread on fruit

Never leave home unprepared. Pack a snack sack of fresh fruit, veggie sticks, nuts, dried fruit, or a little cooler with a smoothie or salad. If you're traveling far, plan ahead and find out where the nearest raw food or health food store is in the area where you will be. Websites such as www.happycow.net are a great place to start.

BEING SOCIAL

Eating socially is a huge part of all cultures, and it can be very stressful for some to assimilate a new diet with the traditions and expectations of friends and family.

* If you are going to be a guest in someone's home for dinner, offer to bring something like salad or dessert. Here's your chance to show off your new culinary skills!

* Nearly all restaurants offer a salad on the menu. Ask for avocado and lemon wedges in place of salad dressing, which is usually bottled dressing with hydrogenated oils and preservatives. You can mash the avocado into your salad and follow with a squeeze of lemon.

* If there are no raw food options where you will be eating, opt for the next best alternative. Steamed vegetables, brown rice, or rice noodles with marinara sauce are a few widely available, gently cooked foods.

* Have a predinner before you go out. If you're famished and surrounded by unhealthy food, that's when things may start to get ugly (at least they do for me).

Never:
* Proselytize or judge others for their food choices.
* Make glum faces and say, "I wish I could eat that." You're eating the best stuff on earth; be excited!

TIP: At restaurants, avoid processed table salt by bringing your own sea salt. You can get handy little wooden travel shakers at www.celticseasalt.com.

Meal Planning

It would require a personal chef to make the more complex recipes in this book every day for each meal. The best way to make going raw doable while having a nice variety of different foods in your diet is to:

1. **Plan ahead.** Soaking, sprouting, and dehydrating might seem like a lot to think about at first, but after time it becomes second nature. For instance, recipes that need soaking and dehydrating should be done in the evening so they can be ready the next day, including wild rice, wraps, and snacks. Make double batches of foods that have a longer shelf life. Many of the snacks and desserts last several days. Prepare them on your days off so you have something waiting when you come home tired and hungry from work.

2. Keep it simple. Smoothies, salads, and soups are my first choice for meals because they take only minutes to prepare and the combinations are endless.

Keep it simple by following this plan:

* For breakfast have a smoothie, chia pudding, scone, or granola cereal.

* For lunch have one of the many different salads offered in this book or create your own. You can make the dressing a couple of days in advance, and the salad can be prepared the night before. Just don't add the dressing or cut the avocados and tomatoes (if you're using them) until you're ready to eat.

* For dinner have an entrée or another salad or soup that you've planned ahead for.

* For dessert have something sweet on hand such as ice cream or brownies. I make only one or two desserts a week, and it usually feeds my husband and me the entire week.

SAMPLE 7-DAY MENU

MONDAY
BREAKFAST: Green Smoothie (see page 60)
LUNCH: Raw Power Salad (see page 81)
SNACK: Cheesy Kale Crisps (see page 152)
DINNER: Asian Noodle "Stir-Fry" (see page 117)

TUESDAY
BREAKFAST: Maple-Pecan Granola with Nut Milk (see page 64)
LUNCH: Spiced Carrot–Butternut Squash Soup (see page 89)
SNACK: Chunky Curried Guacamole with celery sticks (see page 102)
DINNER: Broccoli and Mushrooms with Wild Rice (see page 110)

WEDNESDAY
BREAKFAST: Sunshine Smoothie (see page 56)
LUNCH: Thai Green Bean Salad (see page 78)
SNACK: Trail Mix Energy Bar (see page 156)
DINNER: Creamy Tomato Fettuccine (see page 128)

THURSDAY
BREAKFAST: Orange-Cranberry Oatmeal Scone (see page 68)
LUNCH: Simply Splendid Kale Salad (see page 71)
SNACK: Ice Box Chocolate Chip Cookies (see page 141)
DINNER: Vegetable Maki Sushi and Miso Soup (see page 114 and 92)

FRIDAY
BREAKFAST: Seasonal Fruit Salad (see page 70)
LUNCH: Mediterranean Hemp Seed Tabbouleh (see page 77)
SNACK: Zucchini Hummus and Flax Crackers (see page 97 and 150)
DINNER: Garden of Eden Pesto Wrap (see page 106)

SATURDAY
BREAKFAST: Chia Pudding (see page 70)
LUNCH: Beet and Watercress Salad (see page 79)
SNACK: Teriyaki Coconut Jerky (see page 149)
DINNER: Classic Veggie Pizza (see page 118)

SUNDAY
BREAKFAST: Berries and Cream Crepes (see page 66)
LUNCH: Creamy Tomato-Basil Soup with Herbed Cashew Hemp Cheese with Flax Crackers (see page 91, 100, and 150)
SNACK: Spicy Hot Zucchini Chips (see page 152)
DINNER: Vegetarian Homestyle Chili (see page 127)

Looking at Health Holistically

Our body is the sum of many parts, and so is our health. It's physical, emotional, psychological, and spiritual, and if one facet suffers, so do the others. With respect to the physical, diet is the cornerstone, and within diet other factors apply. Here are just a few of the important tenets of good physical health.

THE ACID/ALKALINE BALANCE

The common abbreviation *pH* stands for the *potential of hydrogen* and is a measurement of how acidic or alkaline a substance is. The pH scale goes from 0 to 14: 7 is neutral pH, below 7 is acidic, and above 7 is alkaline. Depending on its mineral content, every food we eat falls somewhere on this scale. In general, most fruits, vegetables, and seeds are alkaline, while most meat, dairy, eggs, beans, grains, and nuts, as well as alcohol and coffee, are acidic.

Our body has a different pH level for blood, urine, cell fluid, saliva, and other digestive juices. The most important of these is blood, which must always stay between 7.35 and 7.45, slightly alkaline. The body has a homeostatic mechanism to help maintain this pH level by depositing and withdrawing minerals from our bones, tissues, and fluids. When we eat a diet that is heavily acidic, our body must buffer it with alkalizing minerals, which are calcium, magnesium, potassium, and sodium. If we have to continually borrow minerals over time, we can weaken our organs, muscles, and bones. Calcium, for instance, is stored in our bones. If we eat a primarily acidic diet, over time we can put ourselves at risk for osteoporosis. In addition, excessive acid (acidosis) can move into our lymphatic system, organs, and fat cells, compromising our immune system and causing weight gain.

Some other health risks associated with high acidity include:

* Lack of energy/chronic fatigue
* Premature aging
* Bladder and kidney problems
* Cardiovascular damage
* Lactic acid buildup and muscle aches
* Headaches
* Skin conditions such as acne, rosacea, and eczema

Interestingly enough, our bodies can become acidic not just from the foods we eat but also from environmental toxins, stress, anger, and negative thinking.

Eating plenty of raw fruits and vegetables can prevent and reverse acidosis, which is why a vegetable juice in the morning, such as Our Daily Greens (see page 63), will start you off on the right foot. Many health experts recommend 80 percent alkalizing foods and 20 percent acidic foods for optimal health. I would also recommend adding plenty of sunshine, laughter, love, and sleep to that equation!

THE IMPORTANCE OF WATER

Clean, pure water is essential for good health. We need adequate fluids to regulate body temperature; flush out toxins; hydrate our skin, lungs, and joints; and transport nutrients and oxygen to our cells, among many other functions.

Unfortunately in our modern age it is becoming increasingly difficult to find good-quality water. In most cities, municipal water contains sodium fluoride, a well-documented neurotoxin that actually weakens bones; accumulates in our thyroid, causing hypothyroidism; impairs the immune system; and has been linked to infertility and bone cancer. Tap water is also treated with chlorine, a disinfectant that has been linked to cancer, and can be contaminated with other toxic substances, including pharmaceutical drugs such as antidepressants and statins.

Many people have turned to bottled water, but even then the quality is questionable. It might be labeled as spring water but is, in many cases, well water or just slightly cleaner tap water packaged in plastic that leaks Bisphenol A (BPA), an estrogenic substance that disrupts our endocrine system. Not to mention the massive number of plastic bottles filling our landfills in leaps and bounds.

So what are the best options? In a perfect world we would drink fresh spring water that has been filtered through miles of the earth's crust. The trend toward foraging for spring water has actually become more popular, especially among raw food circles. The website findaspring.com lists natural springs around the world. Check it out and see if there is one near you.

For the rest of us who don't live near a spring or have the time to forage regularly for one, I recommend a whole-house water filtration system, or at least a kitchen-sink filtration system. There are many good ones out there, so shop around and compare. Just make sure that it can effectively remove fluoride, because many of them actually do not. Most pitcher filters such as Brita do not remove fluoride and remove only a percentage of chlorine and other substances. Consider a reverse osmosis filtration system that also removes fluoride. You can add minerals back into the water by throwing in a small pinch of Celtic sea salt and store it in a large ceramic crock with pieces of rose quartz. Quartz crystals help create negative ions and revert the water molecules back into their structured crystalline form, which is lost during filtration. This makes the water more energized and hydrating. Friends and family often comment on how great the water tastes at my home.

DETOXING YOUR WORLD

Eliminating toxins from your environment is just as important as eating a clean diet.

You could benefit from detoxing:
* If you regularly eat prepackaged or fast food
* If you smoke or have smoked cigarettes
* If you regularly drink tap or bottled water
* If you have taken prescription drugs
* If you have used cosmetics and toiletries that contain chemicals

* If you work in an area that uses chemicals, such as paint shops, hair salons, furniture shops, photography darkrooms, mechanic shops, etc.
* If you commute to work in a metropolitan area
* If you live in a high-smog area (Los Angeles, New York City, or Washington, D.C., to name a few)

Certain environmental issues are slowly degenerating your health. Even though eating raw food is cleansing, we must also try to avoid reabsorbing environmental toxins. Some of the ways we can stay clean are:

* Eat organic, unprocessed foods.

* Use natural cosmetics, perfumes, lotions, soaps, shampoos, hairsprays, etc. Anything you put on your skin will absorb into your bloodstream, so make sure it's all natural. If you can't eat it, I don't recommend putting it on your body.

* Use all-natural house cleaners and laundry detergents. Avoid chemical air fresheners and candles made with synthetic ingredients.

* The air inside your home can be more toxic than the outside air because of furniture treated with formaldehyde and fire-retardant interior house paint; hairspray; and fried-food vapors. Keep your windows open when the weather is warm and get an air filter—or even better, learn how to grow your own fresh air. See "Resources" on page 189.

* Avoid cigarette smoke.

You can assist your body in removing toxins through several holistic methods:

* **Colon hydrotherapy:** Some people report major health improvements when they combine a raw food diet with colonics, such as increased energy, fewer acne breakouts, and an overall sense of well-being.

* **Breathing techniques:** Deep breathing can increase the amount of oxygen that enters our bloodstream, helping our cells move toxins out.

* **Rebounding:** Jumping on a mini trampoline or jumping rope helps keep our lymphatic system moving. The lymph can become stagnant through a sedentary lifestyle.

* **Massage:** Lymphatic drainage massage helps release toxins in the muscles and lymph. What better excuse to treat yourself to a massage than to say it's for your health?

* **Skin brushing:** This technique involves simply taking a coarse, natural, bristled brush and brushing your skin with it for five minutes every day. Start at your hands and feet and brush toward your heart. This helps stimulate the lymphatic system and exfoliate toxins that are released through the skin.

* **Sauna:** Dry heat or far infrared saunas can help toxins exit through the skin.

The subject of detoxing is a book unto itself, so explore the many facets on your own. See "Resources" on page 189 for a listing of some of my favorites.

STRESS AND HEALTH

Life is stressful. Period. We all have to juggle a career, family, and whatever curveballs life throws at us, but it is imperative that we find ways to manage stress. Unchecked, stress can cause hormonal imbalance, weight gain, heart problems, insomnia, impaired immune system, premature aging, anxiety, and headaches, and that's just for starters. It also affects our personal relationships, our happiness, and our relationship with food.

One anecdotal effect of raw food is its ability to calm and bring a sense of well being and clarity. You might have even met some supercool and groovy raw foodists who seem at peace with the world and life in general. In fact, I have yet to meet an uptight raw foodist. But clearly it isn't just the food; it's also the discipline of practicing stress management. When you're not stressed, you can think clearly. If your mind is burdened, your outlook on life can be negatively affected. Here are a few things that, if you can wiggle them into your schedule, can make a big difference in your health and quality of life.

* **Exercise:** Walking, hiking, yoga, rebounding, bike riding, and running all help release feel-good endorphins.

* **Laughter:** It really is the best medicine. It also releases endorphins and lowers stress hormones and blood pressure.

* **Sleep:** Try to get seven to eight hours a night. Work in naps during the day if needed.

* **Meditation and prayer:** Both practices can clear and calm our minds.

* **Sunshine:** Spend ten to fifteen minutes a day getting sun on your arms and legs. If you live in a cold climate, supplement with vitamin D_3. Vitamin D is actually a hormone that supports our immune system, lifts depression, energizes, and balances.

* **Take baths.**

* **Journal.**

* **Garden.**

* **Find a hobby.**

* **Spend time with friends.**

* **Take a break** from your computer, social networking sites, mobile phones, and everything else that keeps you from living in the real world.

Set aside time for yourself every day to do at least one of these things. Schedule it in like you would a business meeting or a doctor's appointment. Life is too short not to enjoy the little things.

· ✳ ·

Many people in today's society are suffering from poor health, obesity, anxiety, and depression due to the toxicity of their environments. The industrialization and overstimulation within our current culture has led to dietary, environmental, emotional, and relational imbalances in many of our lives. The good news is that a growing number of people are actively taking a role in impacting their own health as they are becoming educated about the importance of detoxifying their bodies, minds, and surroundings. Knowledge is power. Equip yourself by learning ways in which you can detoxify your life. It is fully within our grasp to transform and alter the course of our health, personal lives, and the future of this planet.

—*Penni Shelton, author of* Raw Food Cleanse *and director of*
Raw Food Rehab

Glossary

agave nectar: a sweet syrup that comes from the agave plant, the same plant that brings us tequila. There is some speculation about how raw it really is, so I suggest using it sparingly. Use clear agave over the brown varieties, which are most likely heated at high temperatures.

arame: a dark, thin noodle-like seaweed. Soak for 5 minutes and rinse before using.

bee pollen: considered to be a superfood among athletes. A very good source of complete protein; high in B vitamins, phytonutrients, and enzymes.

blue-green algae: a type of microalgae that contains an array of vitamins, minerals, enzymes, phytonutrients, and amino acids and is high in chlorophyll. A popular superfood used in smoothies and salads.

Bragg apple cider vinegar: a raw vinegar that works great in dressings and sauces and can be taken with water as a digestive aid.

buckwheat: a gluten-free seed used for raw granolas and cereals and a great source of protein. Buckwheat sprouts should be eaten only in moderation, because they can cause sun sensitivity called fagopyrism.

cacao butter: fat that has been separated from the cacao bean. Used for chocolate and other desserts.

cacao powder: ground cacao beans, also known as cocoa powder. Most supermarkets carry only heated cacao, so find a reputable raw brand at health food stores or online. It's the best plant source of magnesium and a great source of amino acids, especially tryptophan, which helps create serotonin and also contains the stimulating alkaloid theobromine. No wonder chocolate makes us feel so happy.

camu camu: a superfood from South America made from the berries of the camu camu bush. Considered to have the highest vitamin C content of any plant.

Celtic salt: a moist, sun-dried sea salt that contains an array of trace minerals.

chia seeds: ancient food of the Aztecs, this gluten-free seed is high in essential fatty acids, complete protein, and fiber.

dulse: a mild-tasting seaweed that you can buy as little flakes or as larger strips. No soaking is necessary, and it can be eaten straight out of the bag. I like storing the flakes in a sugar dispenser to make it easy to sprinkle on salads.

evaporated cane juice: also known as rapadura, this is the least processed form of cane sugar.

galangal: a root similar to ginger but less spicy and more earthy. Used in various Asian cuisines.

goji berries: a rich red-orange berry high in antioxidants that has been used for centuries in Chinese medicine as a powerful tonic herb.

Himalayan pink salt: a prized, high-mineral salt excavated from the Himalayan mountains.

Irish moss: a seaweed that has been used by herbalists for centuries as an expectorant and digestive aid, but has now become invaluable for its use in desserts and sauces as a substitute for gelatin. It must be rinsed very well and then soaked for 12 hours before use.

jicama: a sweet and crunchy root vegetable from Mexico similar to a potato; it can be enjoyed raw.

kamut: an ancient grain high in protein and minerals that is easier to digest for people with wheat sensitivities.

kelp granules: a great salt substitute, or useful if you want to give something a fishy taste, such as a Thai sauce or "tuna" salad.

kelp noodles: a sea vegetable product that resembles glass noodles. They take on the flavor of whatever sauce you use them with. Rinse well before using.

lecithin: a powder usually made from soy that is useful as an emulsifier and thickener in recipes. Look for non-GMO brands.

maca: a Peruvian root that is dried and ground into a flour. Known as an adaptogenic superfood, it helps support the hormonal, nervous, and cardiovascular systems.

Medjool date: a soft and chewy date that has a lovely caramel-type flavor and a higher water content than other varieties.

miso: a fermented Asian condiment usually made from soybeans and rice. I use chickpea miso from Miso Master because it is soy free and has a very nice, mild flavor.

nama shoyu: a fermented and unpasteurized soy sauce.

nori: these are the most popular of seaweeds and are used for making sushi rolls. All nori sheets are toasted unless marked otherwise.

nutritional yeast: a food supplement that is high in B vitamins. Gives raw food dishes a cheesy flavor, similar to that of Parmesan cheese.

palm sugar: an unrefined sweetener made from the sap of coconut trees. Has a brown sugar–like flavor, is high in minerals, and can be used in place of evaporated cane juice.

psyllium husk powder: a fiber-rich dietary supplement that is also used as a thickener in recipes.

rejuvelac: a fermented beverage made from wheat and rye berries.

rye berries: a low-gluten cereal grain that can be sprouted or used in essene breads. Can be used to make rejuvelac.

seaweeds: high in minerals and a great source of iodine, which is essential for the thyroid; they are a great addition to salads and soups.

spirulina: an ancient single-celled blue-green algae high in protein, vitamins, minerals, enzymes, phytonutrients, and chlorophyll.

stevia: the leaves of the stevia plant have been used as a sweetener for centuries. It's extremely sweet with a bitter, licorice aftertaste. An acquired taste but favorable for those who are avoiding sugar.

superfoods: foods that have a very high ORAC value (oxygen radical absorbance capacity—the method to measure antioxidant content) as well as other qualities that are extraordinary. They're considered to be more like whole food supplements. Some are very delicious, such as cacao and goji berries.

tahini: a delicious paste made of sesame seeds. A good source of calcium.

tamari: a fermented and gluten-free soy sauce appropriate for people with wheat allergies.

tamarind: an exotic sweet and sour fruit from Asia often used in salad dressings and sauces. Look for it as a seedless paste in Asian food markets.

wakame: a hearty green seaweed. Soak it in water for and then rinse before using.

wheat berries: hulled wheat kernel used to make rejuvelac. Can be sprouted and used in essene breads.

wild jungle peanuts: an ancient, heirloom nut from the Amazon. They do not contain aflatoxin, a toxin made by a mold found in American peanuts.

yacon syrup: a sweet, almost molasses-like syrup that comes from the yacon root.

Zante currants: a small, sweet variety of black grape. Dried, they are a mini version of the common raisin.

Resources

Ingredients and Equipment

Vita-Mix
www.vita-mix.com

Navitas Naturals
www.navitasnaturals.com

Living Light
www.rawfoodchef.com

The Raw Food World
www.therawfoodworld.com

Raw Guru
www.rawguru.com

One Lucky Duck
www.oneluckyduck.com

Excalibur Dehydrator
www.excaliburdehydrator.com

Organic Vanilla Bean Company
www.organic-vanilla.com

Find a Spring
www.findaspring.com

Lifestyle and Community

Renegade Health
www.renegadehealth.com

Give It to Me Raw
www.giveittomeraw.com

Living and Raw Foods
www.living-foods.com

Natural News
www.naturalnews.com

Raw Food Planet
www.rawfoodplanet.com

Raw Vegan Radio
www.rawveganradio.com

Books

Detoxing

Clean by Alejandro Junger

Detox Your World by Shazzie

Raw Food Cleanse by Penni Shelton

The Raw Food Detox Diet by Natalia Rose

Gardening

All New Square Foot Gardening by Mel Bartholomew

How to Grow Fresh Air by B. C. Wolverton

Western Garden Book of Edibles by Sunset Books

Recipes

Ani's Raw Food Essentials by Ani Phyo

Everyday Raw by Matthew Kenney

The Fruits and Greens Diet by Raw Chef Andi

I Am Grateful by Terces Engelhart

The Lazy Raw Foodist's Guide by Laura Bruno

Raw Food Made Easy by Jennifer Cornbleet

Raw Food, Real World by Matthew Kenney and Sarma Melngailis

The Raw Food Revolution Diet by Cherie Soria

RAWvolution by Matt Amsden

Sprouting

Sprout Garden by Mark Mathew Braunstein

Diet and Health

The 12 Steps to Raw Foods by Victoria Boutenko and Gabriel Cousens

The 150 Healthiest Foods on Earth by Jonny Bowden

Becoming Raw by Brenda Davis and Vesanto Melina

The Body Ecology Diet by Donna Gates

The China Study by T. Colin Campbell

Crazy Sexy Diet by Kris Carr

Diet for a New America by John Robbins

Green for Life by Victoria Boutenko

High Raw by Kevin Gianni

Raw Emotions by Angela Stokes-Monarch

The Raw Food Lifestyle by Ruthann Russo

Superfoods by David Wolfe

The Thrive Diet by Brendan Brazier

Blogs

We Like It Raw
www.welikeitraw.com

Rawmazing
www.rawmazing.com

Loving Raw
www.lovingraw.com

Raw on $10 a Day (or Less!)
rawon10.blogspot.com

Raw Reform
www.rawreform.blogspot.com

Raw Food, Right Now!
www.rawfoodrightnow.blogspot.com

Choosing Raw
www.choosingraw.com

Anarchy in the Garden: Keeping It Punk by Growing Your Own
www.anarchyinthegarden.com

Life on the Balcony: Gardening Tips for Apartment and Condo Dwellers
www.lifeonthebalcony.com

Canarsie BK: Simple Solutions for Living in a Complex World (urban gardening, raw foods, and green living)
www.canarsiebk.com

Raw Food Rehab
www.rawfoodrehab.ning.com

Index

A

advanced glycation end products (AGEs), 15
agave nectar, 30
alcohol, 16, 182
alkaline, 16, 182
antioxidants. *See* phytonutrients.
Ants on a Log, 173
Apple Cider, 63
Apple Cobbler with Maple Cream, 136–137
Asian Noodle "Stir-Fry," 117
avocados, slicing and dicing, 37

B

B₁₂ vitamin, 21, 59, 81
balance, 175, 176
bars. *See* cookies and bars.
Basic Flax Crackers, 150
Basic Nut Cheese, 99
Basic Nut Milk, 56, 58, 79, 160
Basic Raw Chocolate, 141, 147
Basic Vanilla Bean Ice Cream, 139
Basil Vinaigrette, 85
BBQ Sauce, 168
BBQ Veggie Burgers, 122–123, 168
"beegans," 11
Beet and Watercress Salad with Sweet Miso Dressing, 79
Berries and Cream Crepes, 67
beverages. *See also* juices; smoothies.
    alcohol, 16, 182
    Basic Nut Milk, 56, 58, 79, 160
    Blueberry Lemonade, 161
    caffeine, 16
    Coconut Chai Cooler, 161
    coffee, 16, 182
    Mango Lassi, 163
    Red Wine Sangria, 159
    Rejuvelac, 167
    Ruby Red Ginger and Honey Sun Tea, 158
    tea, 16, 68, 158
blenders, 32
Blueberry Cream Smoothie, 61
Blueberry Lemonade, 161
Boutenko, Victoria, 19, 60
Braunstein, Mathew, 50
Brazier, Brendan, 16
breakfast
    Berries and Cream Crepes, 67
    Chia Pudding, 70
    Maple-Pecan Granola, 64
    Orange-Cranberry Oatmeal Scones, 68
    Seasonal Fruit Salad, 70
Brick, Gabrielle, 34
Bright Eyes Juice, 63
Broccoli and Mushrooms with Wild Rice, 110
butters, 28, 178

C

Cabbage Cup, 171
calcium, 12, 21, 59, 68, 70, 71, 97, 110, 182

canned foods, 11, 15
Cellulite Smoother Juice, 63
cheeses
    Basic Nut Cheese, 99
    Classic Veggie Pizza, 120
    Herbed Cashew Hemp Cheese, 100, 151
    Parmesan Cheese, 169
    Pignolia Cheese, 94
Cheesy Kale Chips, 152
Chia Pudding, 70
chiffonade technique, 36
chlorophyll, 19, 49, 60, 84
Chocolate Ganache, 172
chopping technique, 35
Chunky Curried Guacamole, 102
Classic Veggie Pizza, 118–121
coconut basics, 41–43
Coconut Chai Cooler, 161
Coconut-Curry Samosas with Plum Chutney, 124–126
Coconut Kefir, 162, 163
Coconut Yogurt, 163
coffee, 16, 182
condiments, 28
cookies and bars
    Fruit and Nut Bar, 148
    Honey-Almond Macaroons, 173
    Ice Box Chocolate Chip Cookies, 141
    Superfood Chocolate Bar, 148
    Trail Mix Energy Bars, 156
costs, 22–23
Creamy Dill Dressing, 85
Creamy Tomato-Basil Soup, 91
Creamy Tomato Fettuccine, 128–129
Crispy Seasoned Onion Rings, 153, 168
Crossman, Andrea, 59
Cucumber Gazpacho, 90

D

Dandelion Salad, 72–74
Dark Chocolate Brownie Chunk Ice Cream, 140
dehydrators, 33–34
desserts. *See also* ice cream.
    Apple Cobbler with Maple Cream, 136–137
    Basic Raw Chocolate, 141, 147
    Fresh Summer Fruit Tart, 133
    Fruit and Nut Bar, 148
    Ice Box Chocolate Chip Cookies, 141
    Mexican Spiced Brownies, 134–135
    Orange-Chocolate Mousse Parfait, 130
    Superfood Chocolate Bar, 148
    White Chocolate Cherry Cheesecake, 142–144
detox, 18, 21, 22, 62, 183–184, 186
diabetes, 11, 15, 22, 137, 175
dicing technique, 36, 37

digestion, 11, 13, 17, 18, 34, 45, 56, 62, 63, 162, 164

E

entrées
    Asian Noodle "Stir-Fry," 117
    BBQ Veggie Burgers, 122–123, 168
    Broccoli and Mushrooms with Wild Rice, 110
    Classic Veggie Pizza, 118–121
    Coconut-Curry Samosas with Plum Chutney, 124–126
    Creamy Tomato Fettuccine, 128–129
    Garden of Eden Pesto Wrap, 106, 108–109
    South-of-the-Border Soft Tacos, 98, 103, 105
    Spaghetti Bolognese, 96, 113
    Vegetable Maki Sushi, 114–115
    Vegetarian Homestyle Chili, 96, 127
Enzyme Time Smoothie, 61
extras
    BBQ Sauce, 168
    Parmesan Cheese, 169
    Pico de Gallo, 169
    Sour Cream, 169

F

fasting, 34, 62, 63
Fat-Free Tomato Dressing, 85
fats, 13, 177
fermented foods
    Coconut Kefir, 162, 163
    Coconut Yogurt, 163
    grains, 167
    Kimchi, 166
    miso paste, 13, 20, 30
    as raw food group, 13
    Rejuvelac, 167
    soy, 20, 23, 92
    Traditional Fermented Sauerkraut, 164–165
fiber, 12, 14, 17, 56, 62, 68, 70, 75, 80, 110
food processors, 32
food storage, 23, 29, 41, 47, 50, 68, 85, 134, 144
Fresh Summer Fruit Tart, 133
Fruit and Nut Bar, 148
fruits
    as raw food group, 12
    shopping list, 27, 29
    sun-dried, 29

G

Garden of Eden Pesto Wrap, 106, 108–109
gardens, 23
Garlic Tahini Dressing, 85
genetically modified organisms (GMOs), 20
Gianni, Kevin, 175
grains
    fermenting, 167

as raw food group, 12
shopping list, 28
sprouting, 51
Green Banana Smoothie, 61
Green Energy Soup, 93
green smoothies, 19, 60–61
Ground Veggie Meat, 96, 105, 113, 127
Guacamole Mushroom Caps, 170

H

Heirloom Tomato Carpaccio, 171
Herbed Cashew Hemp Cheese, 100
herbs. *See* spices and herbs.
heterocyclic amines (HCAs), 15
Honey-Almond Macaroons, 173
Honey-Whole Grain Mustard Dressing, 85
hydration, 17, 59, 183

I

Ice Box Chocolate Chip Cookies, 141
ice cream. *See also* desserts.
    Basic Vanilla Bean Ice Cream, 139
    Dark Chocolate Brownie Chunk Ice Cream, 140
    Maple-Pecan Ice Cream, 140
    Strawberry Ice Cream, 139
iron, 12, 21, 59, 148
IronMan/IronMama Smoothie, 59

J

Jicama Fries, 170
Jicama-Papaya-Mango Salad, 75
Juice Feasting, 34, 62, 63
juicers, 34
juices, 62–63. *See also* beverages; smoothies.
julienne technique, 35

K

kale, destemming, 37
Kimchi, 166
knives
    chef's knives, 31
    chiffonade technique, 36
    chopping, 35
    destemming, 37
    dicing, 36, 37
    julienne technique, 35
    mincing, 35
    slicing, 37
Kouchakoff, Paul, 15

L

leafy greens, 12
leukocytosis, 15
Liver Cleanse Juice, 63
livestock, 24
Living Light Culinary Institute, 7, 9

M

mandoline slicers, 38–39
Mango Lassi, 163
Maple-Pecan Granola, 64

Maple-Pecan Ice Cream, 140
maple syrup, 30, 52
Marinated Yellow Summer Squash, 80
meal planning, 176, 177, 179–180, 181
Mediterranean Hemp Seed Tabbouleh, 77
Mexican Seasoned Veggie Meat, 105
Mexican Spiced Brownies, 134–135
Mexican Wild Rice, 98
mincing technique, 35
Mint Chocolate Chip Smoothie, 58
miso paste, 13, 20, 30
Miso Soup, 92
Muesli Bowl, 172

N
nuts and seeds
    butters, 28
    cashews, 30
    as raw food group, 12
    shopping list, 28
    soaking, 46–47
    sprouting, 50

O
oils, 13, 28, 42
Orange-Chocolate Mousse Parfait, 130
Orange-Cranberry Oatmeal Scones, 68
organic foods, 23–24
Our Daily Greens Juice, 63, 182

P
packaging, 24
Parmesan Cheese, 169
pasteurized foods, 11, 47
Peaches & Greens Smoothie, 61
pH balance, 182
phytonutrients, 17, 56, 71, 76, 84, 89, 102, 129
Pico de Gallo, 169
Pignolia Cheese, 94
Piña Colada Smoothie, 57
Pizza Crust, 118
Pizza Sauce, 120
planning. See meal planning.
pregnancy, 59
processed foods, 14, 15, 22–23
protein, 18–19, 20
Protein Crunch Mix, 81, 154

R
Raw Power Salad, 81
Red Wine Sangria, 159
Rejuvelac, 167
Romaine Wraps, 170
Ruby Red Ginger and Honey Sun Tea, 158

S
salads and dressings
    Basil Vinaigrette, 85
    Beet and Watercress Salad with Sweet Miso Dressing, 79

Creamy Dill Dressing, 85
Dandelion Salad, 72–74
Fat-Free Tomato Dressing, 85
Garlic Tahini Dressing, 85
Honey-Whole Grain Mustard Dressing, 85
Jicama-Papaya-Mango Salad, 75
Marinated Yellow Summer Squash, 80
Mediterranean Hemp Seed Tabbouleh, 77
Raw Power Salad, 81
Seedy Avocado-Tomato-Corn Salad, 82
Simply Splendid Kale Salad, 71
Spinach Pear Salad with Maple-Cinnamon Vinaigrette, 76
Sunflower Seed Dressing, 85
Thai Green Bean Salad, 78
Vietnamese Salad, 83
Wild Arugula Orange-Fennel Salad, 84
salts, 28, 179
sample menu, 181
Savory Smoothie, 61
Seasonal Fruit Salad, 70
sea vegetables, 13, 92
Seaweed Salad, 171
seeds. See nuts and seeds.
Seedy Avocado-Tomato-Corn Salad, 82
Sesame-Ginger Dipping Sauce, 114
Shelton, Penni, 186
shopping, 23, 27–29
side dishes. See soups and sides.
Simply Splendid Kale Salad, 71
Skin Saver Juice, 63
slicing technique, 37
smoothies. See also beverages; juices.
    Blueberry Cream Smoothie, 61
    Enzyme Time Smoothie, 61
    Green Banana Smoothie, 61
    green smoothies, 19, 60–61
    IronMan/IronMama Smoothie, 59
    Mint Chocolate Chip Smoothie, 58
    Peaches & Greens Smoothie, 61
    Piña Colada Smoothie, 57
    Savory Smoothie, 61
    Smooth Pear Smoothie, 61
    Sunshine Smoothie, 56
snacks
    Ants on a Log, 173
    Basic Flax Crackers, 150
    Cabbage Cup, 171
    Cheesy Kale Chips, 152
    Chocolate Ganache, 172
    Crispy Seasoned Onion Rings, 153, 168
    Fruit and Nut Bar, 148
    Guacamole Mushroom Caps, 170
    Heirloom Tomato Carpaccio, 171

Honey-Almond Macaroons, 173
Ice Box Chocolate Chip Cookies, 141
Jicama Fries, 170
Muesli Bowl, 172
Protein Crunch Mix, 81, 154
Romaine Wraps, 170
Seaweed Salad, 171
Spicy Hot Zucchini Chips, 152
Stuffed Date Rolls, 173
Sun-Dried Tomato and Herb Flax Crackers, 151
Superfood Chocolate Bar, 148
Sweet & Spicy Candied Pecans, 155
Teriyaki Coconut Jerky, 149
Trail Mix Energy Bars, 156
social eating, 178
Soria, Cherie, 6–7
soups and sides
    Basic Nut Cheese, 99
    Chunky Curried Guacamole, 102
    Creamy Tomato-Basil Soup, 91
    Cucumber Gazpacho, 90
    Green Energy Soup, 93
    Ground Veggie Meat, 96, 105, 113, 127
    Herbed Cashew Hemp Cheese, 100
    Mexican Wild Rice, 98
    Miso Soup, 92
    Spiced Carrot-Butternut Squash Soup with Pine Nut Cream, 89
    Spinach-Walnut Pesto and Pignolia Cheese-Stuffed Mushrooms, 94
    Thai Coconut Soup, 86–88
    Zucchini Hummus, 97
Sour Cream, 169
South-of-the-Border Soft Tacos, 98, 103, 105
soy, 20, 23, 92
Spaghetti Bolognese, 96, 113
Spiced Carrot-Butternut Squash Soup with Pine Nut Cream, 89
Spicy Hot Zucchini Chips, 152
Spinach Pear Salad with Maple-Cinnamon Vinaigrette, 76
Spinach-Walnut Pesto and Pignolia Cheese-Stuffed Mushrooms, 94
spiral vegetable slicers, 40
sprouts
    grain sprouts, 51
    jar method, 48–49
    as raw food group, 12
    sunflower seeds, 50
    tray method, 50
Stokes-Monarch, Angela, 21, 63
storage, 29
Strawberry Ice Cream, 139
stress, 185–186
Stuffed Date Rolls, 173
substitutions, 52

Summer Cooler Juice, 63
Sun-Dried Tomato and Herb Flax Crackers, 151
Sunflower Seed Dressing, 85
Sunshine Smoothie, 56
Superfood Chocolate Bar, 148
superfoods, 13, 61, 76, 148
sweeteners
    agave nectar, 30
    as raw food group, 13, 30
    shopping list, 29
Sweet & Spicy Candied Pecans, 155

T
tea, 16, 68, 158
Teriyaki Coconut Jerky, 149
Thai Coconut Soup, 86–88
Thai Green Bean Salad, 78
tools
    blenders, 32
    checklist, 40
    dehydrators, 33–34
    food processors, 32
    juicers, 34
    knives, 31
    mandoline slicers, 38–39
    spiral vegetable slicers, 40
Traditional Fermented Sauerkraut, 164–165
Trail Mix Energy Bars, 156
transition, 175–178

V
vanilla beans, 46–47
vegans, 11
Vegetable Maki Sushi, 114–115
vegetables
    as raw food group, 12
    shopping list, 27
Vegetarian Homestyle Chili, 96, 127
Vietnamese Salad, 83
vinegars, 30

W
water. See hydration.
weight loss, 6, 7, 14, 21, 63, 175
wheat, 22, 23
White Chocolate Cherry Cheesecake, 142–144
Wignall, Judita, 6, 7
Wild Arugula Orange-Fennel Salad, 84
wild rice, 30, 44, 98, 103, 110

Z
Zucchini Hummus, 97

Acknowledgments

First and foremost, thank you to my wonderful husband, Matt, who encouraged me to follow my raw food endeavors, who unbegrudgingly changed his entire diet, and with a smile, ate plate after plate of my culinary trials and errors. You made my food look amazing through your camera lens and were my full-time cheerleader during the writing process. Thank you for your continual love, patience, and support.

Much thanks to my friend Brandon Holschuh for getting the ball rolling with Quarry Books and to my wonderful editor, Rochelle Bourgault, who made it all happen. Many thanks also to Maureen Baker for her assistance.

Thank you to my food stylist, Sienna DeGovia, for being so amazing, and to my assistants, Cora Liposchak and Ryan Benno, who were a huge help on the photo shoots.

Thank you to all my food testers who volunteered their time, energy, and resources to try out my recipes.

Thank you to my teacher and raw food chef extraordinaire, Cherie Soria, for sharing her vast knowledge and for being such an inspiration and encouragement to me.

A huge thank you to Vita-Mix for generously donating equipment.

Thank you to Wesley Crane and Julie Morris at Navitas Naturals for supplying much-needed ingredients and support.

Thank you to Cole Meeker at Artisana Naturals for your friendship and continued support.

About the Author

Judita Wignall is a commercial actress, print model, and musician from Los Angeles. She discovered the healing power of raw foods four years ago after health challenges made her reassess her diet and lifestyle. Her passion for great-tasting food, holistic health, and wellness brought her to Living Light Culinary Institute, where she became a certified raw food chef and instructor. In between her many creative projects, she continues to teach classes, coach, and cater for clients around the country. www.rawjudita.com

About the Photographer

Matt Wignall is a fine art photographer from Los Angeles. www.mattwignall.com